£11·95

D1476762

RECOLLECTIONS OF THREE REIGNS

the male courtiers has. Is this a good thing? It was conceived a good idea after the war to democratize the monarchy by making ex-service men courtiers, to bring a sense of realism to the throne. In practice this meant the new equerries, unused to the world of the court, insecure in their social position, never dreamt of talking to the late King George VI or Prince Philip and the Queen as Ponsonby would have done. This is a loss which will not be righted until the payment of equerries is commensurate with their importance as advisers to the Queen of England and the head of the Commonwealth. Apparently some merchant banker gave idiotic, parsimonious advice on this issue: a change would appear to be a priority which would establish better relations between the royal family and the public. Even Ponsonby in his time was badly paid: this luckily led him in his old age to writing. Only once did royal displeasure fall on his head: he published certain letters of the Empress Frederick, his ownership of which the royal family were not too happy about. But such was his charm that all was soon forgiven and forgotten and he was made a peer by his master of twenty-five years, King George V, shortly before his death.

Antony Lambton

Introduction

Sir Frederick Ponsonby, later Lord Sysonby, was born into the royal household. His father had served Queen Victoria for many years as a senior and principal secretary. His mother, Mary Bulteel, had been a lady-in-waiting to the Queen before her marriage. Early in life he was called back from India to join the family. He was an efficient, courteous and charming courtier with an excellent sense of humour. As the reader will see he didn't mind standing up to his employers if he thought that they were wrong, and although this momentarily annoyed them they realized the value of having an adviser who was not afraid of speaking his mind.

He shone as a conversationalist and raconteur and his wit often kept King Edward VII and King George V amused. For the last twenty-one years of his life he was keeper of His Majesty's Privy Purse. He became an equerry to Queen Victoria in 1894 and remained for over forty years in the royal household. His ability to see the comic side of royal life comes out in the following pages in which he never displays the pompous conceits usually associated with royal biographers and diarists. His independence, and the affection he inspired, enabled him to influence two kings to make the right decisions and to change their minds. I have omitted his recollections of King George V – a patchy work which had not been finally revised when he died.

The book therefore covers the first fifteen years of his service with Queen Victoria and Edward VII, of whom, in the main, he paints a witty and affectionate portrait. In one way it is instructive as it illustrates changes which may have not been for the better. During the reign of Edward VII and Queen Alexandra, the King's courtiers and the Queen's ladies-in-waiting came from the best families in England. Today, while the status of 'ladies-in-waiting' has not changed, that of

When Major-General Sir Henry Ewart was appointed Crown Equerry in 1894, that is, the official in charge of the stables, it created a vacancy among Queen Victoria's Equerries.

In Charles II's reign, the Groom-in-Waiting was the man who made all the arrangements for the King's journeys and for all the private ceremonies that were not managed by one of the great officers of State. He was the only official who attended the King when he went in the Royal Barge. This post continued to be the pivot of the Royal Household until Queen Victoria's reign when, in order that Her Majesty should be attended by adherents of the Government in office, all grooms were made Parliamentary grooms, that is to say, they were members of Parliament. As this entailed their coming in and going out with the Government, it was obviously impossible to make them responsible for arrangements of any description, and so the Equerries took their places while the Grooms became purely ceremonial officers.

Whenever a vacancy occurred in the Household all sorts of suggestions were invariably put forward by members of the Royal Family, but Queen Victoria had definite ideas of her own. On this occasion she determined to do what she thought would please my father, Sir Henry Ponsonby, who had been her Private Secretary for a great many years, and appoint me as a surprise for him. She therefore telegraphed direct to me in India without telling him, and the first he heard of it was a telegram from me asking if I could refuse. He might have thought I was too young at the age of twenty-seven for such a post. He, however, replied that I could not well refuse and so I accepted. Later I heard there were two subsidiary reasons for Queen Victoria's deciding to offer me the appointment. I had acted in a French play at Osborne and she thought I should be useful to her in France as I spoke French well. Secondly, there were questions relating to her Indian attendants which she thought that I, fresh from India, would be able to deal with.

As my duties as Equerry to the Queen only occupied four months in the year, I had to serve as a soldier for the remaining eight. In those days this presented no real difficulty, but, despite the fact that most of my four months' duty as Equerry had to come out of my leave, I soon incurred the wrath of my commanding officer on account of my absences from the battalion. He suddenly became very democratic, and said that it was monstrous that I should count as an ordinary officer in the battalion when I was so often away. But as my position was laid down in regulations, he could do no more than make caustic remarks on the subject.

When I was gazetted Equerry it shocked the military mind, and the chronicler in the *Guards' Magazine* pointed out that this was a solitary instance of a Lieutenant succeeding a Major-General.

The secret of the unique position Queen Victoria held in this country was that she was the personification of the virtues that were most admired at that time. She was, so to speak, the Mother of Europe, and her influence was felt in most European countries. To have discussed political problems with Prime Ministers and statesmen of every party during her long reign alone gave her an immense advantage in her later years, to say nothing of the fact that, while Governments went in and out, she remained at the head of affairs and insisted on being kept fully informed not only on all domestic affairs, but also about everything connected with foreign affairs and the Dominions.

Sir Henry Campbell-Bannerman★ told me that once, when he was trying to persuade her to withdraw her opposition to some measure proposed by the Liberal Government, she said to him, 'I remember Lord Melbourne using the same arguments many years ago, but it was not true then and it is not true now.' He said he felt like a little boy talking to his grandmother.

I was always struck with the facility with which she expressed herself on paper. She never seemed to want for a word and there is no doubt that very few women of her time would have been able to write the letters and telegrams she did. Her grasp of foreign politics was quite remarkable, but in this she had been well schooled from her youth, first by 'Uncle Leopold', the King of the Belgians, and later by the Prince Consort.

I remember Lord Esher† telling me that when he and Arthur

★ (1836–1908); Secretary for War, 1886 and 1892–5, when allegations that the War Office was insufficiently supplied with cordite led to the fall of the Rosebery Government; became leader of Liberal Party in 1899 and later Prime Minister, 1905–08.

† Reginald Baliol Brett, 2nd Viscount Esher. No mere recital of offices held does justice to this remarkable man. On the one hand, he was an intimate friend of Queen

Benson had been asked by King Edward to publish her letters,* they at first decided to publish only those letters which had been written up to the death of the Prince Consort, as they were under the impression that he had inspired her writings and that after his death the letters would deteriorate. When, however, they looked at the later letters, they found to their surprise that, so far from deteriorating, they became even more interesting. Although possibly they lost in literary style, they gained in interest as they were far more forcibly expressed and full of character.

In 1894 I did my first month's waiting as Equerry. Although I had known a great many people in the Royal Household in my youth, I was quite ignorant of how things were done; nor did I know how the ordinary routine work was distributed. Although I was at an age when I thought I knew everything, I was mercifully shy, and therefore probably not bumptious. My first waiting began at Osborne, where I found Lord Bridport,† Lord-in-Waiting, aged eighty, General Sir Michael Biddulph, Groom-in-Waiting, aged seventy, General Sir Lyndoch Gardiner, aged eighty, and my father, Sir Henry Ponsonby, the Queen's Private Secretary, who was over seventy. They must have disliked a young man of twenty-seven being thrust on them, but they never showed it and all were kindness itself.

I soon found that the duties of the Junior Equerry were nil. He had to ride by the Queen's carriage if two Equerries were wanted, or if the Senior Equerry were unable to do so, but otherwise he was not expected to take any part in the routine work. I therefore contented myself with making copies of all the orders issued by the Senior Equerry and picking up as much as I could of the way the machine worked.

The Queen kept very much aloof from the Household generally and everything had to be written to her. Even Sir Arthur Bigge did his work this way. There was, of course, the advantage of having the

Victoria, King Edward VII and King George V; on the other, he was closely in touch with Lord Rosebery, Mr Balfour and Sir Henry Campbell-Bannerman. His advice was greatly valued by both sides. In other fields, his most important work was connected with army reform, in which he was a strong supporter of Lord Haldane.

* *Selections from the Correspondence of Queen Victoria*, edited by Viscount Esher and A.C. Benson, was published in 1907.

† Alexander Nelson Hood, 1st Viscount Bridport; grandson of 1st Earl Nelson (Horatio Nelson's brother).

Queen's decisions on paper, but it gave quite an unnecessary amount of work. The ladies of the Household naturally saw more of the Queen than the men, but as regards myself, I never saw her except when I was invited to dinner. It was a great crime to meet her in the grounds when she was out in her pony chair, and of course we all took very good care that this should never happen. If by any unlucky chance we did come across her, we hid behind bushes. Sir William Harcourt, walking one day with my father, looked up and saw the Queen coming down the path. There was only one small shrub near, and Harcourt asked whether he was expected to hide behind that, but as he was six feet four inches high, my father suggested that the wisest thing to do was simply to turn back.

Unfortunately I had displeased the Queen when I had first been appointed, and it took several years before I was forgiven. She had before I joined the Household a Khitmagar named Abdul Karim, whom she had promoted to be Munshi. There was nothing wrong about this because he was a Mohammedan, and a Munshi, or teacher, is not very high up in the Indian world. Abdul Karim, however, gave himself great airs on his promotion and alleged that his father was a Surgeon-General in the Indian Army. The Queen thereupon telegraphed to me while I was still in India and instructed me to go and see the father at Agra. I stayed with General Morton there and of course took steps to obey the Queen's commands; I found that the man was not a Surgeon-General but only the apothecary at the jail. I saw him and we had a conversation in Hindustani, but as my knowledge of the language only enabled me to talk platitudes about the weather and the beauties of India, it was not a very inspiring conversation.

When I returned home and took up my appointment the Queen asked whether I had seen Abdul Karim's father and I replied I had done so, but that I had found he was only the apothecary at the jail at Agra. She stoutly denied this and thought I must have seen the wrong man, but I maintained that I was right.

I was under the impression at first that I had merely cleared up some point under discussion, but I soon found that it had been a singularly inopportune moment to have blurted out this undoubtedly true statement of fact.

The Queen had begun to show the Munshi letters and despatches from India and it was found that he had an undesirable friend who was in touch with the disorderly elements in India. Quite obviously this might have led to trouble and therefore Sir Arthur Bigge, Sir

Fleetwood Edwards,★ Sir James Reid,† and Colonel Davidson‡ thought it their duty to protest. The result was that the Queen was very angry and did not hesitate to show her displeasure by never speaking to any of them. It was then that I came on the scene and, quite unconscious of the situation, told her that the Munshi's father was not a General but apothecary at the Agra jail. The Queen very much resented this proof of the Munshi's untrustworthiness being brought forward at such a moment and was therefore particularly vexed with me.

She asked Prince Louis of Battenberg§ to come to Osborne and put things right, and no better man could have been chosen. At first he entirely took the Queen's side and maintained that she had a perfect right to show what letters she chose to the Munshi, but when he learnt the other side of the question, and saw the letter from Lord George Hamilton,★★ the Secretary of State for India, to the effect that it would be impossible for him to send highly confidential papers in future to the Queen if she showed them to the Munshi, he saw that what seemed a trivial matter might have very dangerous consequences. He told her frankly that in India the Hindus would very much resent a Mohammedan being placed in the position of adviser, and that the Indian Princes would not be able to understand a Munshi being placed in such a responsible position.

The result of all this was that the Queen abandoned the idea of letting the Munshi see confidential papers, but in order to show her complete confidence in him she said in future he was to be called her Indian Secretary.

To mark her displeasure towards me, the Queen did not ask me to dinner for a year. I spent a month with her at Cimiez, where there were only Sir Arthur Bigge, Sir James Reid and Sir William

★ Sir Fleetwood Isham Edwards. Assistant Keeper of the Privy Purse and Assistant Private Secretary to Queen Victoria, 1878–95; Groom-in-Waiting, 1880–95; Keeper of the Privy Purse to Queen Victoria, 1895–1901; Extra Equerry to Queen Victoria and King Edward VII, 1888–1910. Died 1910.
† Sir James Reid, 1st Bart. Resident Physician to Queen Victoria and Physician-in-Ordinary to King Edward VII and King George V. Died 1923.
‡ Later Colonel Sir Arthur Davidson. Groom-in-Waiting to Queen Victoria and later Equerry-in-Waiting, 1895–1901; Equerry, Assistant Keeper of the Privy Purse and Assistant Private Secretary to King Edward VII, 1901–1910; Extra Equerry to King George V and Equerry to Queen Alexandra, from 1910. Died 1922.
§ Later 1st Marquess of Milford Haven. First Sea Lord, 1912–14.
★★ Son of 1st Duke of Abercorn.

Carington,★ besides myself, to ring the changes on, and yet I was never once invited to dinner, nor did I speak to her during the visit. The day she left for England it was my duty to stand on the reverse side of the carriage in case some unauthorized person should attempt to approach, and there I stood in a tall hat and frock-coat. Just before she got out of the carriage she turned to me and said, 'What a pity it is to leave Nice in such beautiful weather!'

This attitude lasted for a whole year and then, although I was by no means forgiven, I was invited to dinner occasionally.

★   ★   ★

Osborne House was mid-Victorian in decoration and some of the rooms were quite startling in their ugliness. Lord Rosebery once said that he thought the drawing-room was the ugliest room in the world, until he saw the drawing-room at Balmoral.

Everyone came down to breakfast and then we all went to our work. This was not easy in my case as I had nothing to do, but I went to the Equerry's room where I had a writing-table, and having read the newspapers, wrote private letters. At noon the Queen went out and the members of the Household all went for a walk, but it was like a lunatic asylum as everybody went alone in different directions. At two o'clock we all assembled for luncheon, where the Master of the Household carved at one end of the table and the Equerry at the other. I had never done much of this and at first my slices of meat were only fit for the workhouse, but by degrees I gained a certain proficiency in the art. These luncheons were always very amusing as there was much wit among the older men. At three the Queen went out driving and again all the members of the Household went walking by themselves. At five the ladies had a big tea, but the men had tea in their several rooms. There was little or nothing to be done till dinner, when we all dressed up in knee-breeches and stockings. All the old men wore breeches which came down to the ankle and were buttoned there. It was supposed to give the same impression as stockings. In most cases they fitted so badly that they resembled the more ancient peg-topped trousers. Lord Salisbury, who as Prime Minister constantly came down to dine and sleep, had such ill-fitting breeches that they looked

★ Sir William H.P. Carington. Groom-in-Waiting and later Equerry to Queen Victoria, 1880–1901; Comptroller to the Prince of Wales, 1901–10; Keeper of the Privy Purse to King George V from 1910. Died 1914.

like ordinary trousers.

The silence in the house was almost oppressive at dinner-time, and those who were asked to dine with the Queen solemnly walked down the corridor with mosaic floors and statues talking almost in a whisper. Sometimes the men were wanted to join the Queen's dinner-party, but if they were not they adjourned to the billiard-room where smoking was allowed.

All this seemed to suit the members of the Household who were over seventy, but I soon found it didn't suit me. In summer I took to bathing before breakfast and swam from a bathing barge where the Royal children were taught to swim later in the day. In the afternoon I rode about the grounds, which were, however, ill-suited for riding as there was little grass. The Household had luncheon separately, but a certain number always dined with the Queen. One of the footmen, who was noted for his cockney accent and lack of good manners, conveyed the Queen's wishes with regard to dinner by putting his head in at the door of the Ladies-in-Waiting drawing-room and saying, 'All what's 'ere dines with the Queen.'

The Queen had a rooted objection to smoking and even disliked reading letters written by anyone who had smoked when writing. Once I received a message from her asking me not to smoke when decyphering telegrams because the official box in which I sent her the decoded telegram smelt strongly of tobacco.

No one was allowed to smoke in any part of Osborne House where the smell might possibly reach the Royal nostrils; this was odd because all her family smoked like chimneys. Originally a smoking-room had been built outside in the garden, a most inconvenient arrangement, as it was unconnected with the house and smokers when it was wet had to walk in the rain to get to it. Later smoking was allowed in the billiard-room, but of course, not in the Household dining-room.

Smoking at Windsor necessitated a very long walk for the guests, as the billiard-room, which was the only room in which smoking was allowed, was a long way off. In conceding the billiard-room to smokers the Queen thought she was really doing all that was necessary. If any gentleman wished to indulge in the disgusting habit of smoking he should go as far away as possible. Many years earlier the Queen had to tackle the difficult problem of smoking. It was when Prince and Princess Christian* were married and he came to

* Prince Christian of Schleswig-Holstein married Princess Helena Victoria, Queen Victoria's third daughter.

Balmoral. The Queen heard to her horror that he smoked. It was not so bad as if he drank, but still it was a distinct blemish on his otherwise impeccable character. The Queen, however, decided to be broad-minded and actually to give him a room where he could indulge in this habit. A small room was found near the servants' quarters which could only be reached by crossing the open kitchen courtyard, and in this bare room was placed a wooden chair and table. She looked upon this room as a sort of opium-den. Later when Prince Henry of Battenberg married Princess Beatrice★ he induced the Queen to alter this barbarous smoking-room, and although she insisted on its being more or less in the servants' quarters, it could be reached without going out of doors, and it was suitably furnished with armchairs, sofas, and writing-tables.

At Windsor the Queen remained in the drawing-room till about eleven and then the guests were allowed to retire to the billiard-room to smoke. A procession was formed and after a long walk the guests reached the smoking-room. A page had to sit up to conduct them to their bedrooms, but often his services were dispensed with when the guests had been at Windsor before.

One night Baron D'Estournelles de Constant,† who was later known as 'L'Ange de la Paix', came to dine and sleep. He said he knew his way and therefore would not require the services of the page. He remained up till one o'clock having an interesting discussion with someone whose bedroom happened to be in quite another part of the castle. The two said 'Goodnight' and D'Estournelles went off to his bedroom. He started well and went up the stone staircase flanked on each side by armoured figures both on foot and on wooden horses, and he found his way quite correctly into St George's Hall, a long gallery nearly three hundred feet in length. In those days the castle was lighted at night by little oil lamps with a circular glass shade, placed in niches in the wall. According to modern standards they gave a miserable light, sufficient to anyone who knew his way, but D'Estournelles didn't. At the end of St George's Hall there were two doors on each side of the throne and, although no real attempt was made to disguise the doors, the woodwork was made to look like the panelling in the rest of the hall. He should have tried the right-hand door, but it happened to be closed and so he went through the

★ Fifth daughter of Queen Victoria.
† A prolific writer on peace and member of the two Hague conferences.

8

left-hand door which was open. After trying different doors he found himself in the chapel and then in the vestry, which was clearly wrong. So he returned and tried other exits from St George's Hall, always to find himself, like *Alice through the looking glass*, back again eventually in St George's Hall. After a long perambulation he decided to return to the billiard-room and start again, but he never succeeded in finding the right door from St George's Hall, and curiously enough never came across any of the night watchmen. When two o'clock came he abandoned the search, collected some rugs and mats, and made himself as comfortable as he could on one of the sofas in the State gallery adjoining the Waterloo gallery. There he slept till the next morning when one of the housemaids came across him, and feeling sure he had been drunk the night before, went off and brought a policeman. He explained the whole thing, but he could see by their faces that neither the policeman nor the housemaid believed a word of his story.

★ ★ ★

The Equerries lived at Barton Manor, a farm-house about a mile from Osborne House. It was quite comfortable, but it necessitated a brougham being ordered to take them to dinner and bring them back to bed. It would have been difficult to walk in knee-breeches and stockings, especially on a wet night. The house was filled with oil paintings, which were really first-rate and which later proved to be valuable. Apparently the Prince Consort had bought the whole collection of pictures from some house when everything was sold. Osborne House itself was filled with pictures and statues, good, bad, and indifferent. One night Harry Legge★ and I were waiting in the hall for the clarence that was to take us down to Barton, and I wanted to show him how statues were usually on a pivot to enable you to turn them any way you fancied. I went to the marble statue of Psyche about five foot high on a pedestal and gave it a twist. Apparently it was not on a pivot but it had a circular base which had the same effect. Instead of turning round it fell slowly forward on top of me and I put my hands up and tried to push it upright again. Harry Legge, who was no weakling, came to help me and we tried till we were purple in

★ Later Sir Harry Legge. Equerry-in-Waiting to Queen Victoria, King Edward VII and King George V, 1893–1915; Paymaster to the King's Household, 1915–20. Died 1924.

the face to save it from falling. I had no idea that a statue was such a heavy thing, but all we were able to do was to prevent it crashing down and being broken into a thousand pieces. I strained my back in my efforts and bruised my head, while Harry Legge hurt his hand and arm before finally letting it down gently on the floor. We then found that although we had managed to prevent it being smashed, one of the wings of Psyche was chipped. Obviously the thing to do was to get it back on its pedestal before anyone noticed the wing was chipped. We rang and eventually got two footmen, both of them powerful big men, but in powdered hair and red livery which was not intended for manual labour. We tried to raise the statue but all we could manage was to get it two or three feet off the ground. As for getting it back on its pedestal, it was clearly out of the question, so having turned the lights out and told the footmen to report the matter early next morning, we drove off to Barton and so to bed. The next morning a mass of men came and managed to get the statue upright, but they said they could not get it back on its pedestal without a small crane which was generally used for this purpose. All idea, therefore, of hushing up this unfortunate accident was at an end, and I had to see Princess Beatrice and ask her to tell the Queen. I felt like a housemaid confessing to a broken teacup.

I was in disgrace the following day and the Queen wished to show that she did not at all approve of my breaking statues. Princess Beatrice told me after dinner that the Queen had quite understood it was an accident, but intended to send a message to all the Household that 'they must not touch the statues and certainly not play with them'. This message was duly conveyed to all the ladies and gentlemen, but Lady Lytton,* who had not heard about my accident, was mystified at receiving a message that in future she was not to touch the statues and certainly not to play with them, and could make nothing of it.

★　★　★

At Balmoral the Queen had only a small Household – just enough to do the ordinary work. The Lord-in-Waiting never went there and the Groom-in-Waiting went rarely. The Equerry-in-Waiting did the

* Widow of 1st Earl of Lytton and daughter-in-law of novelist. Sister of Lady Ampthill.

work of the Master of the Household and generally superintended everything.

The Gillies' Ball at Balmoral in those days was bacchanalian, but the hard drinking was supposed to take place late so that if anyone was the worse for drink no one should know of it. But as it began at seven and the Queen's dinner was usually about nine, those who had to wait at table had already been dancing for two hours. On one occasion it was a warm evening and, no doubt without being in the least drunk, some of the servants who waited were in rather a hilarious mood. The piper did not seem to mind whether he made a good shot at the glass when he poured out the wine, and some of the footmen were rather slap-dash in their methods. The piper only made one or two really bad shots, but there were loud crashes when someone outside dropped the plates and dishes. Two old pages eventually ran the dinner and firmly eliminated all those who could not be trusted in the dining-room. The Queen had been brought up to think that everything was excusable on the night of a Gillies' Ball, and that it was up to her to keep the conversation going so that no one would remark anything. She was most amusing and told stories which were really quite funny. She went back to the earlier part of the century and described how badly things were done in those days.

Being Junior Equerry, I was always sent for if any extra jobs had to be done. One day the Duc de Nemours* came to luncheon with the Queen; after luncheon she had had enough of him, but as his train didn't leave till 3.30, Princess Louise, Duchess of Argyll,† was asked to talk to him. Unfortunately she had an engagement and so he was shown into a sitting-room while I was sent for. I was told to talk to him in French for forty minutes, and as I had never seen him before, I began to wonder how I was going to fill up the time. It was far worse for the old man to have a young Englishman thrust on him and in all probability he would have been far happier sitting by himself. When I came in I found him seated in an armchair, and he told me to come close as he was deaf. He seemed relieved, however, to find I could talk French.

Having touched lightly on the state of the weather and been met with no response, I came rather to a standstill. I was fairly well up in French politics, and, as it was not very difficult to guess what his

* Second son and heir of King Louis Philippe.
† Queen Victoria's fourth daughter.

views were, I plunged boldly into the situation in France. Setting alight to a barrel of gunpowder would be a comparatively mild proceeding compared to the effect of my conversation on this old man. He got very excited, jumped up from his chair and paced up and down the room with one hand in his coat, while he shook the other in my face to give emphasis to his statements. He shouted at me that it was heartrending to see France in the hands of unscrupulous men who were only working for their own interests; what France really needed was a man who had the good of the country at heart and who would work disinterestedly for the State and not for purely selfish motives. He compared the politicians of years ago with those in power at the present day, needless to say to the detriment of the latter. I roused him to a state bordering on frenzy when I asked what he would do if he were Prime Minister. He roared that nothing would induce him to mix himself up with such *canaille*, but if he did then he would carry out the following reforms. It suddenly dawned on me that forty minutes was far too short for this interview and it was with the greatest difficulty that I got him downstairs and into the carriage. What I think happened was that he never got a chance of saying all this to the Queen and so determined to unload it on me, in the hopes that I would repeat it.

On another occasion I was sent for suddenly to prevent an unpleasant brawl taking place between two foreign diplomatists. Señor Cipriano del Mazo, the Spanish Ambassador, having been accused of attacking the Spanish Government in some speech he had made, had been recalled and was to be replaced by Señor di Casa Valentia, who was his chief accuser. Cipriano del Mazo, furious at this indignity, said that if he ever met di Casa Valentia he would spit in his face and insult him. So we were told that when they both came to Windsor, one with the letter of recall, and the other with letters of credence, they were on no account to meet. Cipriano del Mazo came down early, but unfortunately missed his train back to London so that he was still in the castle when Señor di Casa Valentia arrived. I happened to be in the corridor at the time and Lord Edward Pelham-Clinton dashed at me and told me to take Cipriano del Mazo into one of the rooms and invent any excuse I could think of. I grasped at once what had happened. I seized him by the arm and told him I particularly wished him to see a picture in one of the adjoining rooms. Determined at any price to prevent any spitting, I almost pushed him through the door and shut it. He seemed rather surprised at my haste, but enquired which picture it was I wanted him to see. I pointed to one and said, 'We have never been able to find out for certain who it was of and who it was by.' But he said, 'I see clearly the name Winterhalter on the picture.' This was rather a facer for me, but I merely said, 'Ah! but is it by Winterhalter? That is the point!' The poor man was completely puzzled and proceeded to examine the picture carefully through his glasses. He probably thought I was drunk or mad, but mercifully a page came in and announced that the carriage was ready to take him to the station.

The Queen was very particular about people writing their names in her Birthday Book. She took the last volume of this about with her wherever she went and on occasions it had been mistaken for the Bible. Everyone who visited her had to write their name, and it became a mass of names of celebrities and nonentities all mixed up together. Mercifully the German Secretary, Herr Muther, was in charge of this book and had to keep the index, which he did indifferently well. When he was away or the Queen was abroad, one of the Equerries was responsible for this most tiresome book.

Sir Harry Legge was once the Equerry at Osborne in charge of the book, and a Siamese Princess came to see the Queen. He knew he would have to obtain her signature and so took the book to her while she was waiting to see the Queen. He asked her what day her birthday was, but this apparently conveyed nothing to her. To make it clearer he said, 'On what day were you born?' and she replied, 'On the ninth waxing of the moon of the season Pyatto in the year San Yow.' Now the whole point of the Birthday Book was that people should write their names on their birthdays, but as he didn't feel equal to spotting this date in the Christian calendar, he thought it safer to ask her to write on a separate sheet of paper.

When I went with the Queen to Aldershot for the big review in 1897 it never occurred to me that I was in charge of the Birthday Book; in fact I didn't even know that it had been brought to Aldershot. The Queen gave a dinner of about forty to all the Generals, Colonels of Battalions, and principal Staff Officers, and I never even saw the book, much less thought of asking anyone to write in it.

The next morning the Queen was leaving for Windsor and I thought I would go for a ride before breakfast. I got up at 6.30 and was just starting out at seven when I received a note from the Queen (written the night before) in which she said she presumed I had got the signatures of all those who dined. I was flabbergasted. The Queen was leaving at 10.30 and the troops were to line the road. To attempt to go round Aldershot in a carriage would take too much time, and so I determined to play the mountain to their Mahomets. I sent away my horse and summoned all the orderlies. There were luckily plenty: four on horses, four on bicycles, and four on foot. I sat down and scribbled notes to all the guests of the previous night and sent them off by degrees as soon as I had written them. I then found that the Brigade of Guards had already started off for Pirbright, and this meant I should be five signatures short. In about forty minutes, Generals, Colonels, etc., arrived at full gallop imagining that the Queen was sitting waiting with the Birthday Book. By 9.30 all had written except the five at Pirbright. I therefore wrote with my humble duty reporting I had all the signatures except the Guards'. The Queen seemed satisfied with this, but sent a message to say I must get the other signatures as soon as possible.

My other adventure with the Birthday Book occurred at Nice. Sarah Bernhardt came to act at the theatre there, and the Queen was pressed by several people to hear her recite. At first she refused as she doubted Sarah Bernhardt's code of morality being quite what it should be, but eventually she agreed to receive Sarah Bernhardt in the drawing-room at the Hotel Regina. It was a great success and the Queen was delighted with the performance of a small play, *Jean Mari*.

I instinctively felt this was a case for the Birthday Book, and after the Queen had left the drawing-room I produced the book and asked Sarah Bernhardt to write her name. She startled me by insisting on kneeling down on the floor to write. Then she took up nearly the whole of one page by writing 'Le plus beau jour de ma vie' and signed it with a flourish.

I felt I had done my duty nobly and when a message came from the Queen asking me whether I had got Sarah Bernhardt's signature I sent the book in with pride for the Queen to see. To my surprise I got no marks. First of all it was the wrong book, and I ought to have used the artists' book, and secondly, I ought to have prevented her taking up the whole page. I was told that the Queen was much put out at this, but in any case I was to get Sarah Bernhardt's signature in the artists' book. By the merest chance I heard that she was leaving Nice for Marseilles that night after the performance in the theatre, so there was only one thing to do, and that was to catch her before she left; but this was not as easy as I imagined, as I found out that she never saw anyone before going to the theatre. I therefore had an early dinner and took a stall for *La Tosca*. After the first act I went round to the box-office and said I wished to see Madame Sarah Bernhardt, but the man, who no doubt had often to grapple with many others who had the same wish, replied with a pitying smile that it was hopeless to try and see her, and hinted that I had better fasten my affections on someone else. It was impossible to argue with a busy man who kept on being interrupted and so I contented myself with asking to see her secretary, and after some trouble he said he would arrange this.

As soon as the next *entr'acte* began I returned to the box-office and after an interminable delay the secretary came, and although polite was very short in his answers. So I had to play the Queen and said, 'Je viens de la part de Sa Majesté La Reine d'Angleterre.' He at once was all over the place and took me to the back of the theatre, where I found in a sort of antechamber a lot of people waiting for a chance to see Sarah. But the Queen's name worked like a talisman, and I was taken at once to her dressing-room, where she received me most cordially. There were two dressers, two sort of ladies-in-waiting, the secretary, and another whom I took to be the lover. I explained my errand, and she said in her *voix d'or*, 'Je l'ai déjà écrit.' I replied that this was so, but I had been commanded to obtain her signature in another book, and I murmured something about its being 'plus intime'. She said certainly she would write, but although the whole party looked everywhere, there was no ink. The lover did find a property inkstand and an old split quill, but no ink. There was nothing to do but to come back during the next *entr'acte*, and the secretary was told to get busy and procure some ink and a pen. Accordingly I sat through the next act and returned, not without difficulty, to her dressing-room. The ink and pen were produced and Sarah wrote her name, but of course there was no blotting-paper. I was so anxious that she should not see the other signatures that as soon as she had written I tried to take away the book. 'Un moment que ça sèche,' she said, and before I could stop her she glanced at the other signatures where several well-known artists' names appeared. The spell was broken. She handed back the book to me with a shrug of her shoulders. She understood.

When the Queen went for a drive in London she always drove in an open landau with one footman and a Highlander up behind, four horses with postilions, two outriders in front, and two grooms in rear. In addition two Equerries in tall hats and frock-coats rode on either side of the carriage.

Once when I was riding with her, an American in a hansom came along behind us, but it was an unwritten law that no carriage of any sort might pass her. I heard an altercation going on and finally the American shouted to the cabman, 'I don't care if there are forty Queens, I have to catch my train and I'll give you a sovereign if I do so.' Not unnaturally the cabman determined to earn his tip and whipped up his horse into a hard gallop to pass the procession in front. Green, one of the grooms in rear, however, thought this should not be allowed. He had been one of the whips of the Quorn and was a finished horseman. He cantered along the side of the hansom till he came to a side street; then he got the cab-horse by the head and turned him to the right smartly, giving him a flick with his whip as he left. The horse galloped down the street and disappeared, while the American was apoplectic with rage.

★　　★　　★

In literature the Queen's taste was said to be deplorable, and although she had little time for reading she never liked the works of the great authors. I remember a discussion taking place once at Balmoral between Queen Victoria and the Empress Frederick on the subject of Marie Corelli. The Queen said she would rank as one of the greatest writers of the time, while the Empress thought that her writings were trash. I was seated at the other end of the large dining-room table and therefore had not, unfortunately, heard the commencement of the discussion. The Empress suddenly called across the table to me and asked me what I thought of Marie Corelli. Quite unconscious of the fact that the Queen was an admirer of this authoress, I replied that her books undoubtedly had a large sale, but I thought the secret of her popularity was that her writings appealed to the semi-educated. Whereupon the Empress clapped her hands, and the subject dropped with startling suddenness. It was not till afterwards that I learnt how I had put my foot in it.*

Queen Victoria had far too much character and individuality to have good taste. Apart from the creators of art, the majority of human beings acquire by degrees good taste by sinking their own individual likes and dislikes and adopting the suggestions thrust on them by experts. Now although the Queen had every desire to encourage art

* A common admiration for Marie Corelli was one of the few sentiments shared by the Queen and Mr Gladstone.

generally, she invariably refused to be influenced in any way by other people's opinions, and having very fixed ideas of her own she clung to what she liked.

★   ★   ★

The Queen usually crossed the Channel in her yacht, the *Victoria & Albert*, escorted by torpedo-boats, and the crowds of people who came to see her pass were quite phenomenal. At Folkestone there were some thousands of people, but they could have seen little or nothing as no one was allowed near the Royal yacht, and on the pier there was a guard of honour and band with the General and his staff. Sometimes the Queen crossed in an ordinary steamer and every possible arrangement for her comfort was made. The only disadvantage of this was that the boat was crammed with both English and French railway directors and managers who thought it was their duty to accompany her. The Queen always insisted on a covered gangway being rigged up on the Royal yacht so that the crowd should not see her being carried in her chair, but with an ordinary steamer this was not possible, and an uncovered gangway was used. It was, however, usually so steep that no one would have expected an old lady to walk up it. At either Cherbourg or Boulogne there was a dense crowd of people who waved and cheered. The British were not popular at the time with the French, but I never saw anything but enthusiasm for the Queen. On the pier was a beautiful red velvet and gold lace tent for her to sit in, with a guard of honour of the French Army, while a host of Generals, Admirals, and officials hoping to be presented were drawn up near the tent. What with the band playing and the crowd continually cheering vociferously, it was difficult to hear anything. We travelled comfortably by train across France, but in those days the washing arrangements were very sketchy. I usually got the courier to telegraph to some station and order a jug of hot water to be ready to be placed in my carriage. This enabled me to wash and shave so that on arrival, when I donned my frock-coat and tall hat, I looked presentable.

We usually stopped at Cannes for five minutes to allow the Prince of Wales, the Duke of Cambridge,★ or any other member of the Royal Family who happened to be there to board the train to meet the

★ Queen Victoria's cousin; Commander-in-Chief of the British Army, 1856–95.

17

Queen. At Nice the whole town turned out and lined the streets from the station to the hotel. There were four regiments of infantry and a battery of artillery to keep back the ever enthusiastic crowd. At the station the Préfet, the Mayor, the General, and a host of men in evening clothes and tall hats were assembled.

The usual routine at the hotel was that the Household had their meals separately as in England, but one or two were invited to join the Queen's dinner. The English hours were kept: breakfast at half past nine, luncheon at one, and dinner at a quarter to nine. There was always a French guard mounted on the hotel with two officers, and this arrangement of meals was apt to upset them as they usually had their *café au lait* at six, *déjeuner* at eleven, and dinner at six.

★　　★　　★

In May 1899 I married, having waited three years. The Queen had strenuously opposed the marriage, giving as her reason that a man always told his wife everything and therefore all her private affairs would get known all over London. Colonel and Mrs Kennard not unnaturally thought me a poor match for their beautiful daughter, and so, faced with all this opposition, we felt unable to publish our banns. But after three years we determined to insist on fixing the date. Colonel and Mrs Kennard at last gave their consent, but the Queen's opposition was more difficult to overcome. It was Miss Phipps who undertook to persuade the Queen that after three years' waiting she should withdraw her opposition. Eventually I was told I might marry, but I was to understand that I should never have a house given to me.

★　　★　　★

The Queen's eyesight became worse about 1898, when she first began to mistake people. The first time I noticed the difference was at Balmoral when before leaving the room she said, 'Where is Fritz?' Before I could interpose, Lord Balfour of Burleigh,★ who was six-foot-five and weighed sixteen stone, came forward with a smile and a bow, not having heard what she said. The Queen, supposing him to be me, asked him how his mother was, which startled him considerably as his mother had been dead for years. Another time she

★ Alexander Hugh Bruce, 6th Lord Balfour of Burleigh.

18

thought Lord William Cecil,* who was standing by the door, was me, and congratulated him on his good shooting. It was particularly unfortunate as he had missed a stag while I had got two, and of course he thought she was ironical; but she suddenly realized her mistake and sent for me.

No one was really kinder to bad shots as a rule than she was, although the head stalker came in every night to tell her exactly what each person out stalking or fishing had done. She always pretended not to know the result of the day's sport and asked for information. Prince Francis Joseph of Battenberg, who was a very bad shot, unlike his brother Prince Henry, unfortunately didn't know this. Having been out stalking, he proceeded to give a rambling account of his day's sport, quite unconscious that the Queen knew every detail. All would have been well if he had left it at that, but he went on to say that it was a pity everything was so badly done and that the stalkers did not know much about stalking. Then the Queen turned on him and rent him. She asked him how many shots he had had, and when he replied he could not remember, she asked whether he had had seven, and had missed them all. She asked how far the stags were when he fired and he replied that he was no judge of distance, whereupon she said, 'I suppose about a hundred yards.' It then dawned on him that she knew exactly what had happened and he shut up like an umbrella. I was a very indifferent but keen fisherman, and as the Queen was always told about every day's fishing she was under no delusion about my piscatorial powers. One night she asked me what sport I had had, and when I replied that I had caught nothing, she said, 'Not a very good fisherman, I fear.'

In 1898 the Neumanns† took Invercauld, the Farquharsons' place, which is a few miles from Balmoral, and when the Prince of Wales came up to stay with the Queen they invited him to a deer drive. I was also included amongst the rifles.

Everything went wrong. In the first place the deer refused to be driven in the proper direction; whether this was sheer bad luck or owing to the lack of skill on the part of the keepers it is difficult to say. Deer when they are conscious of being driven invariably go straight back through the beaters and therefore it has to be done in a subtle manner. Whatever the cause was, the drive that lasted two hours

* Son of 3rd Marquess of Exeter.
† Later Sir Sigmund Neumann, 1st Bart.; prominent in Edwardian banking circles.

proved a failure and no one got a shot. The Prince of Wales, who knew the difficulties, took it with great equanimity and made light of it, but when the luncheon proved a fiasco, it was quite a different matter. Neumann, full of apologies for the failure of the drive, led us off to luncheon. He had made all the arrangements himself so that there should be no mistake. We walked down a path in single file and he assured us that it was not far. After half an hour's walk we came to a wood and Neumann explained he had chosen this sheltered spot in case it was a windy day. It seemed an ideal place but there were no signs of anything to eat. He told us to wait a moment while he looked about and, like a hound who is trying to pick up the scent, he circled round and round but with no success. The Prince of Wales, who by that time was getting very hungry, began to make very scathing remarks about rich men undertaking things they knew nothing about and ended by shouting suggestions to the wretched Neumann, who was still scouring the countryside at a trot. I then went after Neumann and asked if I could help. He produced a copy of his orders and said he had looked out the place on a map, which didn't seem to help much. While we were talking he caught sight of a shepherd and raced off after him. The shepherd explained that the place he had written down was over five miles off and that the one we had come to was differently pronounced, although spelt very similarly. The problem was how to get the luncheon and the guests together. Neumann begged me to explain the situation to the Prince of Wales and tell him that he would go as fast as he could to get a conveyance if the guests would walk as far as the road and wait there. H.R.H. on hearing the explanation called Neumann every synonym for an idiot, but urged by hunger he agreed to walk to the road, which took us about half an hour. It was then past two and there, on a heap of stones, we sat silently waiting for a conveyance. Conversation was at first tried, but eventually we all relapsed into gloomy silence. It was past three when a wagonette arrived and we all bundled in. When we did find the right place we thought the luncheon was the best we had ever eaten. But it was too late to have another drive in the afternoon and we returned home.

★　　★　　★

The Duke of Connaught was commanding the troops in Ireland and in addition to his official residence occupied a house in Phoenix Park which Lord Iveagh★ lent him. It was a lovely house with oak and tapestry and the Duchess of Connaught and Princess Patsy preferred it to the official house. One day I walked with Princess Beatrice to pay a visit to the Duke and Duchess of Connaught and rather an amusing incident happened. The Duchess of Connaught, pointing to an old black chair with a high back, said to me, 'That is a most comfortable chair. Do try it.' I ought to have suspected that there was some sell as it was most unlikely that she would wish to have my opinion on a subject like this. I at once sat down, when to my horror some spring worked and two iron clamps came out and closed with a snap, holding me fast. There were roars of laughter in which I joined, although I could not move. Then the Duchess explained that all she had to do to release me was to touch a spring at the back of the chair, and she proceeded to show how easily this was done. 'Come here, Patsy,' she said. 'You know how to do it better than I do.' Princess Patsy went to help and there was much fumbling behind the back of the chair, but still I remained pinned to the seat. 'I am afraid it is broken,' said Princess Patsy, and I had visions of remaining there for days. 'Nonsense,' said the Duchess, scarlet in the face from pushing at every likely place at the back of the chair, while I sat with an idiotic smile on my face pretending I was amused. By now the laughter had quite died away and I had become an extremely tiresome incubus. 'Ring the bell for the butler,' suggested someone; but no one came, the butler having gone out with the Duke. Where were the footmen? One had gone with the carriage, and the other had just been sent off with a telegram. So we had tea, and as the Duchess and Princess Patsy felt responsible for my detention, they brought me every sort of biscuit and cake to pass the time. Meanwhile Princess Beatrice was itching to go, feeling that she was outstaying her welcome, but she hardly liked to leave me still imprisoned. Someone then suggested that the gardener knew the secret and we all cheered up. Princess Patsy offered to go and find him, but minutes passed, the conversation languishing when no gardener appeared. Again I felt like the skeleton at the feast, but after another twenty minutes the gardener appeared and at once touched the right spring. I sprang out of the chair with alacrity in case anything should go wrong again, and when taking leave of the Duchess I said that never again would I sit down on any chair in her house.

★ Edward Cecil Guinness, later 1st Earl of Iveagh.

I had barely taken over the reins of Acting Private Secretary when the situation between England and the Dutch Republics suddenly took a very threatening turn, and the constant cypher telegrams added to my work enormously. The Queen insisted on knowing everything and insisted on her prerogative of reading and approving every dispatch before it was sent off. Sometimes her approval had to be telegraphed to avoid delay. This caused a peculiar position to arise when, early in October 1899, an emergency Cabinet drafted a very moderate and even conciliatory dispatch to President Kruger, which merely recapitulated our demand for the franchise and made no mention of the delicate question of suzerainty. The Queen wished to study this and therefore her approval was not telegraphed immediately. Meanwhile an arrogant telegram from Kruger had been received, peremptorily calling on the British Government to send all troops away from South Africa and practically amounting to a declaration of war.

The question arose what should be done with the conciliatory dispatch that had been drafted by the Cabinet. It seemed out of the question that it should even be considered. Sir Fleetwood Edwards said that according to the Constitution the Queen must approve of a dispatch or alter it, but I argued that this was making an absolute farce of her approval, as she could neither approve nor alter it after Kruger's telegram had been received. We had a long argument and finally it was agreed to submit the matter to Harry Chaplin,★ the Minister in Attendance. He knew little or nothing about constitutional methods as far as the Sovereign was concerned and decided that the best thing he could do was to back up Edwards, because he was the older and more experienced man. Between them they drafted a telegram to be sent to Chamberlain, saying the Queen had approved of the dispatch before Kruger's telegraph had arrived. I pointed out that this was useless, but as it would have to be submitted to the Queen before it was sent I was quite ready to wait until her consent had been received. She knew far more about the Constitution than any of us and would therefore be the best judge, but I asked that both sides of the controversy should be fairly put to her. Edwards therefore saw her and dispassionately stated the question, whereupon she unhesitatingly took the same view as I did and sent back the dispatch to Mr Chamberlain not approved.

When war was declared a few days later I found the Queen in a

★ Later 1st Viscount Chaplin.

bellicose mood after dinner; she seemed all in favour of teaching Kruger a sharp lesson, but later she became lachrymose about the senseless waste of human lives all this might entail.

Troops were dispatched to South Africa with feverish haste, and while some people said we were overdoing the whole thing and sending out too many men, others were of the opinion that we were not sending enough.

★   ★   ★

In 1899 the Queen had started an album for photographs of all the officers killed in the war. It was a sad business writing to widows and mothers and asking for these photographs, but it seemed to give them some consolation. This gave endless work as it was necessary to write a special letter in each case, and sometimes to get involved in a long correspondence. The Queen liked to see all the answers I received, and in addition to this I had to see that the date and circumstances under which every officer was killed were written under each photograph. Mercifully the gumming-in of the photographs was done by an expert, also the writing of the names and particulars, but in order to ensure that no one was forgotten, the lists had constantly to be checked. After a year, the Queen came to the conclusion that the book was too sad to look at, and therefore the living should be added in order to make it less mournful, but as it was obviously impossible to include all the officers fighting, it was decided to confine it to all Generals holding commands in South Africa. This did not give so much trouble, as the same letter did for all.

Not content with this, the Queen wished a special letter to be written to all parents who had four sons or more fighting in South Africa. This was another long business, but really the War Office supplied the names, verified each case, and dealt with masses of letters that arrived claiming a number of sons fighting. At Christmas the Queen had special boxes of chocolate made with her effigy on the lid and these were sent to every officer and man in South Africa. It was a pretty idea, and the personal touch was much appreciated, but I imagine it must have given the Army organizations in South Africa a great deal of work.

Up to the end of her life the Queen continued to take the greatest interest in everything connected with the war, and the sick and wounded were constantly in her thoughts.

Lord Marcus Beresford* was the most spontaneously witty man I ever knew; when he was in good form he would keep people in roars of laughter. There are many stories of his witty repartees, but usually witty remarks said on the spur of the moment are no longer amusing when written down. I remember his trying to play bridge once at Brighton when King Edward was staying with Mrs Arthur Sassoon.† King Edward came in and said, 'Hallo, Marcus, playing cards. I didn't know you knew one card from another.' He replied, 'I know a king when I see one.' Another story that always amused me was when he went to a theatre and on arrival was met by the cloak-room woman who said to him, 'Shall I take your hat and coat, sir?' 'No, thanks,' he said. 'Shall I take your cap and apron?'

When, therefore, Bill Carington organized a night out in London for Sir James Reid, the Queen's physician, he asked Beresford to be one of the party to enliven the proceedings. First there was dinner, then a play, and afterwards supper. After the play was over they decided to walk the short way down the Strand to the Savoy for supper. Reid and Beresford came last of the party, and as they passed another theatre which the audience was leaving there was a smart brougham drawn up at the door with a beautiful woman in it waiting for her husband. Beresford seized Reid before he understood what was happening, pushed him into the brougham, slammed the door and said 'Right' to the coachman, who drove away. Of course, Reid was furious, and after he was finally released told everyone that the beautiful lady had said to him, 'You ought to be ashamed of yourself. You're drunk.' What with hammering at the window to stop the coachman and the lady shouting at him, he had no opportunity of explaining his case. However, the husband, to whom he apologized, had seen the incident and roared with laughter. So it all ended happily.

★　　★　　★

Once in February 1900, the Queen's health not being good, Sir James Reid asked me to take steps to ensure that no bad news should reach her by telegram. I had not found this quite so easy to arrange as I anticipated, for when I told Mr Hiley, the telegraph clerk, to bring me any telegram that might come for the Queen before sending it in to

* Son of 4th Marquess of Waterford.
† At 8 King's Gardens.

her, he replied he had strict orders from her that all telegrams addressed to her were to be sent in at once to her and to no one else. I had spoken in a careless manner so that there should be no suspicion that anything was wrong, but I grasped that I should have to take him into my confidence. I therefore told him the Queen was unwell and that Sir James Reid had impressed on me the necessity of her not being worried by bad news, and I finally wrote down and signed instructions to him enjoining secrecy. However, the next day the Queen recovered, and as no telegrams arrived, all was well.

On January 21st [1901] everything went on much the same as before, but after dinner a long telegram about the war in South Africa arrived and I went off to ask Reid what should be done with it. He said with a grave face that there had been a change for the worse and that he feared that the end might come at any time during the night. I therefore dispatched a mounted groom to summon Edwards and Bigge and I also sent a carriage for the Bishop of Winchester (Randall Davidson). They all came and we had a long consultation and it was decided that the Prince of Wales should be told at once. The telephone in those days for long-distance calls was very uncertain, but after some delay I managed to get on to the Prince of Wales himself, and he decided to come at once by special train.

★   ★   ★

When I came down to breakfast at ten I found somewhat better news about the Queen; the Prince of Wales had returned and the German Emperor had arrived. Although the rest of the Royal Family seemed to resent his coming and no one had asked him to come, he behaved in a most dignified and admirable manner. He said to the Princesses, 'My first wish is not to be in the light, and I will return to London if you wish. I should like to see Grandmamma before she dies, but if that is impossible I shall quite understand.' Nothing could have been better.

The whole house was crammed and even all the houses in the vicinity were full. I expected every minute to be turned out of my bedroom, which was large and comfortable, but no one even suggested this.

When the Prince of Wales went in to see the Queen she became conscious for a moment and recognized him. She put out her arms and said 'Bertie', whereupon he embraced her and broke down completely. Another time during a moment of consciousness she sent for her dog, a little white one, and called it by its name.

About luncheon-time we heard the Queen was sinking and I sent for Bigge and Edwards. A carriage was sent for the Bishop of Winchester and Clement-Smith, the Rector of Whippingham. No change, however, occurred for several hours.

Arthur Balfour arrived and discussed the action of Parliament. He was astounded at the accumulation of official boxes that had taken place during the last week and said it showed what a mass of routine work the Queen had to do. Still there was the point to be considered how the machine could go on without her. Judges, for instance, could not function without a warrant signed by her: all sorts of appointments could not be made without her sanction. He impressed on Bigge the necessity for summoning a Privy Council, no matter what happened. But we all knew it was only a matter of hours.

At about half past six we were told that the end had come. The Duke of Argyll told me that the last moments were like a great three-decker ship sinking. She kept on rallying and then sinking. The behaviour of the German Emperor was beyond all praise. He kept in the background until they were all summoned. The Prince and Princess of Wales, Princess Christian, Princess Louise, and Princess Beatrice stood around the bed, while the German Emperor knelt down and supported the Queen with his arm, while Reid held her up on the other side. The Emperor never moved for two and a half hours and remained quite still. His devotion to the Queen quite disarmed all the Royal Family.

When the news came, Bigge sent and stopped the telegraph wires until the official telegrams to the Lord Chancellor, Prime Minister, Archbishop of Canterbury, Lord Mayor of London, etc., had been dispatched. I was told the scene on the hill down to Cowes was disgraceful. Reporters in carriages and on bicycles were seen racing for the post office in East Cowes, and men were shouting as they ran, 'The Queen is dead.'

As the last death of a sovereign had occurred in 1837, no one seemed to know what the procedure was. We spent the evening looking up what had been done when George IV and William IV had died. A Privy Council seemed urgent, but at first the Prince of Wales refused to go and argued there was no immediate hurry. When Lord Salisbury cyphered to Arthur Balfour that there must be no delay, the Prince consented to go to London the next day.

★　　★　　★

26

The 60th Rifles had been sent for from Parkhurst Barracks to provide a guard over the coffin, and when they arrived and asked for orders no one quite knew what the procedure was. The men had never been taught to reverse arms and the drill book was dumb on the subject. I was appealed to under the misapprehension that I had done this sort of thing before, but I was really very hazy about the subject. A most intelligent and smart captain, however, after consultation with Sir John M'Neill and myself, evolved a ceremonial for relieving the men every hour, as the strong perfume of the flowers seemed to upset them at first, and it was arranged that four men should stand with reversed arms at the four corners while one of the Household should keep watch at the foot of the coffin.

The Duke of Connaught, however, found out that it was the privilege of the Queen's Company, Grenadier Guards, to mount guard over the defunct Sovereign, and a telegram was sent off summoning them at once. They arrived with two officers, St John Coventry and Myles Ponsonby. Coventry was extremely sketchy about the whole thing and simply copied the 60th Rifles. When however, Arthur Lloyd, the Captain of the Queen's Company, Grenadier Guards, came along it was a very different thing and the changing of the sentries became a most impressive sight, all done in slow time. In addition to the Grenadiers one member of the late Queen's Household kept watch. I found this very trying, not only on account of the very strong scent of the tuberoses and gardenias, but because I could ill afford the time. The dining-room was turned into a mortuary chapel and was hung round with curtains and draperies. The coffin was covered with crimson velvet and ermine with the crown in diamonds on a cushion, and the Order of the Royal Standard. The room was lighted by eight huge candles and there were palms round the room in addition to masses of wreaths. It was all gorgeous with colour and most impressive.

The Princess of Wales refused to be acknowledged as Queen and would not let anyone kiss her hand. She said that there could only be one Queen until the funeral and that she wished for the present to remain as Princess of Wales.

King Edward then took charge of the funeral arrangements and had all the difficult points submitted to him for decision. He sent for me and told me he wished me to take charge of all the funeral arrangements at Windsor. He impressed on me that the service at St George's Chapel would be arranged with the Dean by the Lord

Chamberlain, and that I would have nothing to do with that. All I had to do was to arrange the procession and give orders to the troops, police, etc., at Windsor.

I therefore decided to go to Windsor the next morning by the earliest train, and telegraphed to the Mayor, the head of the police, and the Officer Commanding the troops, to meet me. I am not sure that it was a wise thing to put someone in charge of the Windsor part of the funeral who would have to take part in the funeral *cortège* starting from Osborne.

When I arrived at Windsor I went to the Town Hall and discussed all the arrangements with the Mayor. He called in the police officials and everything went well. The officer commanding the troops was luckily David Kinloch,★ a most capable and first-rate organizer, and I went over all the ground with him. We decided that in view of the fact that there would be colossal crowds the procession, instead of going straight from the station to St George's Chapel, should go down High Street, Park Street, and then up to the castle through the gates at the bottom of the Long Walk. I told him that the funeral procession itself was being managed by the Earl Marshal and that, beyond having a few officers available to marshal the procession, he need not trouble about that. As everything seemed satisfactorily arranged I returned to Osborne in the evening. Knollys and Greville had practically taken over the whole of the secretarial work and therefore there was no reason why I should remain at Osborne, but when on my return I asked whether anything had been decided about the funeral at Windsor, I was told that nothing of any sort had come from the Earl Marshal's office about Windsor as they were still concentrating on the London part.

I naturally became anxious. The next morning, Thursday, January 31st, in case it was supposed that I was doing the funeral procession as well as the arrangements of troops, police, etc., I determined to go to London and make sure what was expected of me. A second time I rushed off to London and went at once to the Earl Marshal's office where I found absolute chaos. The Heralds, who claimed the right to manage the funeral under the direction of the Earl Marshal, had little precedent to work on since there had been no Sovereign's funeral for sixty-four years, and being accustomed to work out coats of arms and genealogical tables at their leisure, were swept off their feet with the

★ Later Brigadier-General Sir David Kinloch, 11th Bart.

urgent arrangements for the funeral. There appeared to be no system and everyone was engaged in working out the little bits of detail most suited to their capacity. I asked for the programme of the Windsor part of the funeral and was told that they had not yet begun it. 'We haven't finished Osborne and London yet,' cried one of them. 'But,' I argued, 'has it occurred to you that the funeral starts from Osborne tomorrow?' I suddenly realized that the Windsor part would be a fiasco, and I should be blamed.

Finding everything so confused I asked to see the Duke of Norfolk,★ the Earl Marshal, and here I found a thoroughly businesslike and capable man dealing with telegrams, letters, ceremonials, enquiries from the Lord Chamberlain, Lord Steward, Master of the Horse, telephone messages from the Foreign, India, and Colonial Offices, but quite unconscious that the work he was delegating to his subordinates was not being done. Although he was working like a cart-horse he at once saw me. He was under the impression that a skeleton programme was being made out and that all that was necessary was to fill in the names, but I explained that nothing had even been started. He seemed rather put out about this and explained that the Lord Chamberlain was constantly supplying him with fresh Kings and Princes who were to attend the funeral, and this made any definite printing of a ceremonial impossible. He said that the best plan would be for me to consult Lord Roberts and then make out a skeleton ceremonial for his approval. So off to the War Office I went, but when I got to the Commander-in-Chief's room I was told that Lord Roberts could see no one. I, however, wrote on my card, 'Funeral arrangements – urgent'. I was at once ushered in and I briefly explained that the funeral began at Osborne the next day and that nothing had been decided about the Windsor part. Lord Roberts said that he had nothing to do with the funeral itself, but if it came to giving orders to any troops, I had his permission to give whatever orders were necessary, and say that they were given with his approval.

★　　★　　★

I had to get up very early and put on full-dress uniform. Arthur Davidson had been put in charge of all the funeral arrangements at

★ Henry FitzAlan-Howard, 15th Duke of Norfolk. His efficiency and despatch are further attested by the fact that he was Lord Mayor of Sheffield and Postmaster-General simultaneously.

Osborne, and I must say it was beautifully arranged. Everyone knew what to do and where to go, and it all went without a hitch. We Equerries were to march on either side of the gun-carriage and to assemble at the front entrance of Osborne House. Punctually the bluejackets from the Royal yacht, under Lieutenant Pelly, carried the coffin down the stairs and placed it on the gun-carriage. The Queen's Company, under Arthur Lloyd, marched in single file on either side of the procession and the whole *cortège* moved in slow time all the way to Trinity Pier, where the coffin was placed on board the Royal yacht *Alberta*. It was a lovely still afternoon and the immense crowd was most impressive. At three the yacht started. Battleships and cruisers were anchored in two lines all the way to Portsmouth. The sun was setting in a red sky as we arrived and it was a very pretty sight to see the little yacht *Alberta* going through this avenue of immense ships. She was followed by the *Victoria & Albert*, the *Osborne*, and the Admiralty yacht, but these anchored in the harbour while she went alongside the jetty. I was told to go on board the *Osborne*, where I found a cabin prepared for me.

About seven o'clock King Edward sent for me and I went in a steam pinnace to the *Victoria & Albert*. He said he wished me to undertake the arrangements for the final service in the Mausoleum at Frogmore on the Monday, and he hoped I should be able to have a printed ceremonial ready for him to see on Sunday morning.

There I was at Portsmouth on board the *Osborne* with nothing to refer to, no precedent to go by, and no idea of who would attend this last ceremony. I was to walk with the other Equerries alongside the gun-carriage through London, and yet I had not only to stage-manage the final ceremony, but also to have a ceremonial printed. I was dead tired, having been all day on the go with very little sleep the night before. I realized that the next day all the shops would close early to enable people to see the funeral and that the day after was Sunday. Up to that moment Arthur Davidson had managed everything so well that he had set a very high standard and I felt that there was every possibility of the Windsor part being a fiasco. If in addition to this I mismanaged the final ceremony, what little chance I had of being taken on by King Edward would evaporate.

When I grasped all the difficulties I felt I had undertaken a hopeless task, but of course there was no alternative but to tackle it. It occurred to me that if I was to have anything printed by Monday, the printers must be warned, and I therefore sent a telegram to Oxley, the printer at Windsor, saying I should want a ceremonial printed by Saturday evening and that he was to meet a messenger whom I was sending by an early train and receive from him the written ceremonial. I sent for one of the King's Home Service Messengers and told him to come to my cabin early the next morning, by which time I should have written out a draft. As the King told me that only those who were staying at Windsor would attend the last ceremony, I grasped that it would be quite a different list from that of the larger ceremony through London. The only possible way I could think of to obtain a correct list was to telegraph to the Master of the Household's clerk at Windsor Castle and ask him to telegraph the names of all those who would be staying in the castle. After dinner I retired to my cabin, where I proceeded to write out a ceremonial in suitable language. Under ordinary circumstances I should never have attempted such a thing, but there seemed to be no alternative, and although in some places it seemed rather bald, I succeeded in producing a dignified programme for the printer. Late that night I received a sheaf of pink telegraph forms giving me, as I had asked, the names and precedence of the guests staying at Windsor for the final ceremony. I filled in all the names and sealed up my draft ready for the Messenger.

The next morning, February 2nd, we all landed at Portsmouth in full uniform and went by special train to Victoria Station. The train with the coffin and one or two of the oldest members of the Queen's Household came later. We all stood waiting with the King and the male members of the Royal Family for this train to come in. The coffin was then carried by men of the Coldstream, under Leslie Hamilton, on to the gun-carriage and the procession started through London with the Equerries on either side. The streets were lined all the way with troops and the densely massed crowd was a wonderful sight, most reverent and silent. As we marched in slow time it took quite a long time to get to Paddington, but on arrival the coffin was again taken from the gun-carriage and placed in the train. We were all told off to various carriages, and so to Windsor.

When we arrived at Windsor I at once got hold of David Kinloch, who had done wonders on the very meagre instructions which I had given him. He had arranged everything perfectly and had managed to form up the outline of the procession, leaving plenty of room as he had no idea of the numbers.

As soon as the King and the other foreign Sovereigns had taken up their places (they were to walk this time), I went and asked His

Majesty's permission to start the funeral procession. It had been previously arranged that I should hold up my hand and the band would begin the *Dead March*, while the officer in charge of the gun-carriage would start at the same time. When I received the King's commands to start the procession, I stepped out well to the side so that everyone could see me and held up my hand. The drums at once began to roll and the procession started.

The horses on the gun-carriage had, however, been standing still in the cold for some time, and as the lieutenant in charge never gave the command 'Walk march', the two wheelers suddenly started off before the leaders, and finding an unusually heavy load, began to kick and plunge. Away flew the traces and the gun-carriage remained still. I had contemplated all sorts of things going wrong, but such a mishap had never occurred to me.

Meanwhile the front of the procession, unconscious that anything was wrong, had slowly marched on and the band had already turned the corner when I sent a non-commissioned officer to stop them. I found then that the traces were broken and everyone was trying to get the horses clear while several officers were engaged in trying to devise some makeshift, but naturally the first thing was to inform the King of what exactly had happened. I did so, and on coming away Prince Louis of Battenberg said, 'If it is impossible to mend the traces you can always get the naval guard of honour to drag the gun-carriage.' I went back to the horses where I found that it was contemplated getting two horses only to drag the gun-carriage with the leaders' traces. The general impression, however, seemed to be that this was a most hazardous solution of the difficulty as it seemed very doubtful whether the two horses would be able to drag the gun-carriage up the steep hill into the castle with traces that were only makeshifts, and which might easily snap. Another solution was suggested, and that was that the gun-carriage should go up by the shortest way to St George's, but this I dismissed as it would have meant disappointing a crowd of several thousands.

So I determined to adopt Prince Louis's suggestion and accordingly went a second time to the King and said, 'Have I your Majesty's permission to take out the horses and let the men of the naval guard of honour drag the gun-carriage?' The King said, 'Certainly.' I told the captain of the naval guard of honour to pile arms and bring his men up to the gun-carriage. While he was doing this I went to the officer in charge of the Artillery team and told him to get the horses clear as the men of the naval guard of honour were to take their places. This raised a storm of discussion, all carried on in a whisper. There were several Artillery officers among the A.C.D.s to the Queen who resented very much the orders I had given, and they assured me that all would be well if I would leave things alone. Bigge was particularly angry and told me I was ruining the whole ceremony as I knew nothing about Artillery horses. I replied that I was merely carrying out the King's orders and that I could not allow anyone to interfere. He was furious, however, and went off to expostulate with the King, who merely said, 'Right or wrong, let him manage everything; we shall never get on if there are two people giving contradictory orders.'

So all the men of the Artillery stood sulkily looking on while I went in search of a rope, feeling this was a necessity for the sailors. The stationmaster to whom I applied rushed off and returned with a steel hawser which was all he had. This was, of course, out of the question as it would have cut the men's hands to the bone. The Artillery A.D.C.s were triumphant and said, 'You'll have to come back to the horses after all.' I went to the Officer Commanding the naval guard of honour and explained to him the situation. He said that if he could have the remaining traces of the horses he could manage and I told him to order his men to get them. The men of the Artillery remained looking on while the sailors swarmed round the horses and took off the traces. In an incredibly short time they had got into a compact group and were ready to start.

The whole of this lasted about ten to fifteen minutes, but it seemed to me about two hours. I went off to the King and reported that everything was ready, and having received orders to start the procession, I stepped out for the second time and held up my hand. This time all went well and I returned to my place alongside of the gun-carriage. The procession moved slowly along High Street and Park Street and then turned up towards the castle through the gates at the bottom of the Long Walk. It was very heavy going and the gun-carriage seemed to sink in, but the sailors experienced no difficulty. One of the A.D.C.s called my attention to the brake and said that if no one understood how to work it there might be serious trouble when we descended the steep hill to St George's Chapel. So I moved out of my place and consulted the naval lieutenant, who said he had a petty officer who understood all about the brake, but that if I liked he would place three men on each wheel so that, in the event of the brake not working, there would be no danger of the gun-carriage going too fast downhill. I asked him to do this. But everything went well and I was able to dismiss from my mind all dangers of another mishap and admire the beauty and dignity of the whole procession.

On arrival at the west door of St George's Chapel, the bearer party of the Coldstream took charge of the coffin and carried it into the choir. We all followed in procession and found the chapel crowded with people. It subsequently turned out that the Earl Marshal's people had forgotten to give seats in the choir to anyone, but Sir Spencer Ponsonby-Fane, to whom the Earl Marshal had entrusted the arrangements in the chapel, had grasped that a mistake had been made and had taken suitable people from the nave and placed them in the choir. The service was most impressive and most beautifully sung.

At the conclusion all the Foreign Sovereigns, Princes and Representatives went up to the castle where there was a stand-up buffet, where I was able to get something to eat and drink; but a message that the King wished to see me interrupted my post-prandial moments, and I hurried off to Edward III's Tower, where the King was temporarily lodged. He told me he wished me to do all the arrangements for the final funeral on Monday, and that as the sailors had done so well that day he would like them again to drag the gun-carriage. I ventured to point out to him that the Artillery had been deeply mortified at their failure that day, coming as it did so soon after the experience at Ladysmith when so much had been made of the handy-man taking the place of the artilleryman, and that therefore they would be much hurt if the sailors took their place again. He talked it over for some time and said that he had no wish to hurt the feelings of the Artillery. He quite realized that they were not to blame and that it was only an unlucky accident, but he really thought that the sailors had been most effective and had really added to the dignity of the procession. I, however, pressed my point and finally he said, 'Very well, the gun-carriage will be drawn by the Artillery, but if anything goes wrong I will never speak to you again.'

I was determined therefore that nothing should go wrong and I wrote to Sir Arthur Bigge, Sir Henry Ewart, the Crown Equerry, the Officer Commanding the battery of Artillery, the lieutenant in charge of the Artillery team, the captain of the Queen's Company Grenadiers, and asked them to come to the door of St George's Chapel at six o'clock the next morning, Sunday. I told the Artillery to have their team of horses there, and Arthur Lloyd commanding the Queen's Company to have all his men there. I received charming letters from all of them, but an especially nice and forgiving letter from Bigge saying he was so glad to hear the Artillery were to have another chance and promising to help me in any way he could.

When the printer's proof of the ceremonial for Monday arrived, I took it to the King, who made several small alterations and sent it back to the printer.

Lord Esher, the Secretary of the Office of Works, suggested that we should have a rehearsal of the final ceremony at the Mausoleum. He asked me to order the bearer party and the gun-carriage and horses to be down at the Mausoleum at eleven that night and he would have a box approximately the same size and same weight as the coffin made by the men of the Office of Works ready at the lodge leading to the Mausoleum. We drove down in a carriage and found all the men waiting. It was a pitch-dark night and there was something very ghostly about the lanterns that were carried to light up various points. It was a weird scene and the two bearer parties, one from the Life Guards and one from the Foot Guards, remained motionless on the steps of the Mausoleum. The gun-carriage with the Artillery team was standing at the lodge with the box on it and had been told not to move until ordered to do so. Lord Esher had thought of everything and had told the men that all was to be done exactly as it would be on the Monday. We then began the rehearsal, and the gun-carriage with the sham coffin advanced slowly to the steps of the Mausoleum. It had been arranged that as the coffin was very heavy one bearer party should carry it up two flights of steps and then be relieved by the other bearer party, who would carry it into the Mausoleum.

The first part went very well and the relieving bearer party took over the sham coffin, and when they advanced up the remaining steps, we realized that they would have to place the coffin on the tomb the reverse way to the marble figure of the Prince Consort. We came to the conclusion that this would never do and we halted the men. While we were discussing what should be done, I noticed that although the bearer party consisted of enormously powerful men they were staggering under the weight of the sham coffin, and I suggested that they should put it back on the gun-carriage while we decided what should be done. The sham box coffin was therefore carried back again and placed on the gun-carriage. We discussed whether at St George's Chapel it would be possible to make the change, but Esher pointed out that the space in the choir was small when the chapel was full and it would be difficult and perhaps irreverent to attempt to turn the coffin round the other way. At last we came to the conclusion this would have to done on the steps of the Mausoleum. We made the bearer parties try various methods, not carrying anything but merely walking slowly. When the relief took place the relieving party had to face the other way and slowly turn round before going into the Mausoleum. After one or two rehearsals this somewhat intricate manoeuvre worked perfectly. Eventually everything went smoothly and we dismissed the men. If it had not been for Esher's forethought in having this rehearsal we should undoubtedly have had another fiasco.

★   ★   ★

At 6 a.m. on Monday I again attended a short rehearsal with the horses. It was very cold and we kept them standing ten minutes before moving off, but they behaved perfectly.

After breakfast the King sent for me and I found him in the corridor. The list of Sovereigns and Princes staying in the castle had been telegraphed to me by the clerk to the Master of the Household, but the name of the Duke of Fife★ had been omitted. The curious part of this was that, although the King and several Court officials had seen the draft of the ceremonial, no one had noticed this omission. Unfortunately the ceremonial had been published in the newspapers and everyone was reading it.

I found the German Emperor, the King of the Belgians, and the King of Portugal† standing by the fire all smoking cigars, which rather shocked me as, of course, no one had ever smoked there before. The King was standing a little further down the corridor with the Duke of Fife, and on seeing me proceeded to reprimand me severely. He said that the Duke of Fife's name had been omitted from the list and he could not understand how I could have made such a bad mistake. How could he have any confidence in me when I made omissions of this sort? It was inconceivable to him how anyone like me, accustomed to arrange ceremonies, should have omitted so important a person as his son-in-law.

Naturally, I didn't say a word and the Duke of Fife, who seemed

★ 1st Duke of Fife. Married Princess Royal, King Edward's eldest daughter.
† Don Carlos, King of Portugal since 1889; assassinated with the Crown Prince, 1908.

pleased to hear me abused, walked off satisfied. As soon as he had gone I said I could not apologize sufficiently for the mistake, which of course I ought to have seen and corrected when the proof came, but I reminded him that the proof had been on his table all Sunday and that no one else had noticed the omission. He at once became quite different and, taking me by the arm, said confidentially to me, 'I know how difficult it has been for you and I think you did wonders. I had to say something strong, as Fife was so hurt that he came to me and said he presumed that he could go to London as he was apparently not wanted.'

A curious incident happened at the last funeral ceremony. An officer in khaki came to see me and applied for tickets for the Mausoleum. I told him that no one but the Royal Family would go to the Mausoleum, but I would give him a ticket for the private grounds. He was a dignified gentlemanly-looking man with several medals. I never gave him another thought, but it appeared that in some unaccountable way he stepped out of the crowd and joined the German suite in the procession. They very naturally thought he was connected with the arrangements and took no notice of him. However, I knew nothing of this.

The whole ceremony went beautifully and it was most impressive to see the foreign Sovereigns, headed by the King, walking behind the gun-carriage. When the gun-carriage reached the steps of the Mausoleum the two bearer parties did admirably. There was dead silence, no whispering or hesitation, simply the slow tread of the men. The doors were closed and the service began. Suddenly a voice whispered in my ear, 'Who is the old bird with a beard?' I looked round and saw the khaki officer, who was pointing to the King of the Belgians. I said 'Hush', took him by the arm, led him to the door, and forcibly ejected him. The service was really beautiful and the singing of the St George's Chapel choir was perfect. At the conclusion of the service we all retired, leaving the Royal Family by the tomb. When I got outside I espied my khaki friend and told him what I thought of his conduct. I said his behaviour was disgraceful and that I had not thought it possible that an officer of the Army should push himself forward and intrude in a purely family service like that. I added that I wanted his name and regiment as I should report him to the Commander-in-Chief. He gave me his name and regiment, saluted, and walked away. We walked back to the castle and on the way we were passed by carriages containing the Royal Family and their suites.

When I entered the quadrangle I saw the Royal Family and foreign Sovereigns and Princes talking together at the Sovereign's Entrance, and in the midst of them was my khaki friend. He had apparently come up in a carriage with the German suite. I went off at once, took him by the arm, and much to the relief of the Royal Family, led him away to the gate, where I luckily found a policeman. I sent for one of the detectives and gave him instructions to take the officer to the station and send him off to London. I then wrote to the Military Secretary and reported the incident. It later turned out that the poor man had been invalided home from South Africa suffering from sunstroke and that he was mentally deficient.

★　★　★

Queen Victoria's life was so hidden from the public that all sorts of myths were bound to gain credence. The stories about John Brown, her Highland attendant who died in 1883, were at one time so numerous and so obviously made-up that it hardly seemed worth while to correct them. I thought at first that while they were untrue there might have been some grain of truth in the popular idea that John Brown had been something more than a faithful servant. The story that they were secretly married rested on no foundation whatever, and I asked several people in the Household who must have known the truth, and they all laughed at the idea. Even the old Duchess of Roxburghe, who was generally supposed to have been present at the marriage, told me that the whole thing was a fabrication inspired by people who wished to ridicule the monarchy, and that certainly she had never heard such a thing mentioned. It appears to have originated when a scurrilous pamphlet entitled Mrs John Brown was privately published. Many people who didn't believe a word of it shook their heads and said that there was no smoke without some sort of fire. Although the tale was not generally believed, no one took the trouble to contradict it. Whether there was any quite unconscious sexual feeling in the Queen's regard for her faithful servant I am unable to say, but judging by what I heard years afterwards, of course, I am quite convinced that if such a feeling did exist, it was quite unconscious on both sides, and that their relations up to the last were simply those of employer and devoted retainer.

John Brown was certainly a privileged servant and could do practically what he liked with the other servants. His word was law with them and his relations with the gentlemen of the Household were difficult to define. Like all Scotchmen of that class he never became familiar and as a rule was always respectful but that did not prevent his being an autocrat with the servants. My father, Sir Henry Ponsonby, seems to have got on very well with him, but Brown always treated him with deference and respect. It was, however, not always so with the Equerries. When General Sir John M'Neill was appointed Equerry he was accustomed to command troops, and although the most charming of men with a great sense of humour, was apt to be rather abrupt in his manner with the servants. On one occasion he was in the Equerries' room at Osborne when John Brown came in with a message about some carriages that were to be ordered. After delivering his message Brown remained standing by the writing-table, whereupon M'Neill told him to wait outside and he would send for him when he had written the order. Brown complained that he was over-bearing in his manner and that he had shouted at him as if he was a private soldier. In the evening M'Neill received a letter from the Queen asking him whether he would like a command in India. The one she referred to was quite a small command which would mean his going down and not up in the military world. Unable to understand why he was summarily to be got rid of, he took the letter to my father, who guessed the cause of the trouble and advised him to reply that he would of course be glad to accept any command that Her Majesty was pleased to offer him, but as people would naturally ask why he was giving up his post in the Household, he begged that he might be told the reason he should give. He followed this advice and heard nothing more, as of course the Queen could not give the real reason; but she never spoke to him for some years and so arranged his month's waitings that he never came to Balmoral or Osborne where she might have to speak to him.

Doctor Profeit, the factor at Balmoral, disliked Brown intensely and resented his constantly interfering with local matters, but was in such awe of him that he never dared stand up to him. Still, it was a well-known fact that these two were enemies. When Brown died in March 1883, the Queen, who was quite unconscious of the bad feeling between the two, presented Profeit with a tiny miniature of Brown set in diamonds and made up like a tie-pin. Profeit realized that if he wore this everyone at Balmoral would laugh at him. He therefore hit upon the idea of keeping it in his coat pocket so that when he had to see the Queen he could take it out and put it in his tie, returning it to his pocket when he came away.

General Sir Lyndoch Gardiner, one of the Queen's Equerries, was one of Brown's pet aversions, although he was quite unconscious of the fact. While he treated Brown well, he was a great stickler for adhering to the rigid methods by which things were done in those days, and if a carriage was wanted he insisted on knowing all the facts before he would write the order. On one occasion he came into waiting and on meeting Brown he enquired how the Queen was and what she had been doing lately. Brown replied, 'The Queen's very well. It was only the other day that she said to me "There's that dommed old fool General Gardiner coming into waiting and I know he'll be putting his bloody nose into everything that doesn't concern him".' History does not relate what General Gardiner replied.

The Queen often quoted John Brown and seemed amused by his quaint expressions. At one time the Duchess of Roxburghe and Miss Stopford★ were not on speaking terms and when Miss Stopford was ill, Sir James Reid, the Queen's doctor, suggested that perhaps the Duchess might go and see her. 'Oh dear no,' exclaimed the Queen. 'There would only be what Brown calls Hell and hot water.'

Often the Queen used expressions that had long since passed out of the slang vocabulary of her contemporaries. Once when a picnic was arranged by the members of the Household, the Queen was asked whether the Maids of Honour might go. She replied that they might, although she did not altogether approve of the ladies 'junketing' with the gentlemen.

★　　★　　★

With the funeral of Queen Victoria there passed an age. Naturally the Victorian tradition took some time to die and the new era was not ushered in within a few weeks of King Edward's accession to the throne, but gradually new methods were being introduced into the Royal Household and every department was being overhauled.

For myself there was little change, for soon after the funeral King Edward sent for me and told me he intended to appoint me Assistant Private Secretary and Equerry. This was good news to me as I knew he meant to make drastic changes in the Household, and I felt he must have thought of all sorts of people whom he knew and whom he intended to give some post in the Household.

★ The Hon. Horatia Stopford, a Woman of the Bedchamber.

Soon after his accession the King began to receive alarming accounts of the health of his sister, the Empress Frederick of Germany, and at once decided to go to Cronberg and see her. Her son the Emperor William was to meet him there. To my surprise he decided to take only his physician, Sir Francis Laking, and myself. He had not realized yet that being a King was a totally different thing from being Prince of Wales, and he argued that as he had formerly taken only one Equerry, one would be quite sufficient on this occasion.

I had seen the German Emperor at various times when I was a boy, but the first time I had an opportunity of speaking to him was when he came to Cowes in his yacht. Of course he was at once invited to luncheon by the Queen at Osborne. It so happened that the same day the Duke of Connaught had asked the Officer Commanding a battalion of the Rifle Brigade at Parkhurst Barracks to send over a man wearing the new equipment that was proposed for the Army. He was anxious that the Queen should see this equipment as there had been much discussion about it.

After luncheon we were all asked to come into the drawing-room and bring the man with us. A particularly smart-looking sergeant of the Rifle Brigade arrived and waited outside. We found the Royal Family talking together and at once the Duke of Connaught sent for the sergeant, who came in looking rather uncomfortable in his dark-green full-dress uniform over which various khaki belts and straps had been put. It all looked very odd. The Duke of Connaught walked round explaining the object of the different straps to the Queen, while the German Emperor merely nodded and grunted to signify that he understood the explanations. I thought that this was all there was to be done, but the Emperor had not had his say. He called me up and asked whether I did not think the greatcoat that was rolled up was too high, and whether it would not interfere with a man firing his rifle lying down. Without waiting for an answer he told the sergeant to lie down and get into a firing position. He then proceeded to lie down alongside and point out that even with a Rifleman's head-dress, which was flat at the back, the greatcoat prevented his putting his head back far enough. He maintained that with a helmet or *Pickelhaube* it would be impossible. It was a very hot afternoon and beads of perspiration broke out on the sergeant's face as he found himself lying down in front of the Queen, with the German Emperor lying down beside him glaring at him and plying him with questions without ever giving him time to answer them. However, all this was intended for the Queen's edification and she seemed much amused. The Duke of Connaught merely replied that this equipment was intended for khaki uniform and that obviously it was unfair to judge it when worn with a full-dress uniform.

For the now proposed visit to Germany I entrusted the travelling arrangements both in England and on the Continent to the courier, while all I wanted to know was the time of departure and arrival of the trains. I myself had to give orders to the police. I had to send instructions to the Royal yacht and arrange with the Admiralty to have two escorting cruisers. I had to inform the War Office that no guard of honour was wanted anywhere, and made it clear that no General, Admiral, etc., was expected to be at the port of embarkation. There were a hundred and one little things to think of, but I knew the game pretty well. The journey was to be kept a profound secret, but, needless to say, the presence of extra police and the arrival of the Royal special train gave the public sufficient indication of His Majesty's movements.

We started on Sunday afternoon and I was horrified to find a crowd lining the streets all the way to the station. King Edward was much put out and made caustic remarks about the ease with which he travelled formerly.

We crossed in the old *Victoria & Albert*, and when we were alongside the jetty at Flushing we heard a large number of people apparently singing hymns. I thought this a very proper way of spending Sunday evening, but what I could not understand was why they sang the same hymn over and over again *ad nauseam*. I asked Sir Henry Howard, His Majesty's Minister at The Hague, who came on board as soon as we arrived, and he explained that it was the Boer National Anthem, and that the mass of people who were singing had originally intended to sing it on the jetty, but that owing to his representations, the authorities had kept them outside.

I got to know this hymn very well, as it was sung at several stations at which the trains stopped, but perhaps the most trying was the singing of 'God Save the King' at Duesseldorf. At two o'clock in the morning a girls' school, led by the headmistress, who had a piercing voice, sang the National Anthem. Of course it was too late to take any notice of it as everyone was asleep, but it woke up the whole train. Afterwards the *Daily Mail* referred to this and said that the young ladies were much disappointed at the King not appearing. I wonder if they expected him to come out on the platform in his pyjamas!

We arrived at Homburg, and found the Emperor at the station in very good spirits and most cordial. We drove at once to Friedrichshof and were shown to our rooms. The house is very much like an English country house, a great deal of it having been copied from Flete, the house of the Mildmays in Devonshire. Herr Ihne, the architect, who built it, was half English, and fell in at once with the Empress Frederick's idea of making it like an English country house. The bedrooms seemed quite English except for the stove. Otherwise the house was like a museum filled with a collection of works of art and curiosities.

★   ★   ★

A Minister with whom the King had little in common was the First Lord of the Admiralty, Lord Selborne, and in most naval matters the King preferred the vigorous opinions of Admiral Sir John Fisher.* When King Edward came to the throne Fisher was Commander-in-Chief in the Mediterranean, but in 1902 he became Second Sea Lord, and in 1903 was transferred at his own request to the Portsmouth Command; while holding this office, he began to draft plans for the entire reorganization of the Navy.

It was at Balmoral in October 1904 that I first made the acquaintance of this tempestuous personality. I was going for a walk one afternoon just as he decided on the same form of recreation. I rather fancy he was bored to tears at the sight of me and would have done anything he could to avoid me, but without being rude he could not avoid my company. As we walked on he began by asking me whether I liked dancing. At the time I thought he had chosen the only topic which he imagined would suit my intelligence, but I found later he was passionately fond of dancing. I determined, however, to get the conversation on more interesting topics and I asked him about the row between Archibald Hunter and Hedworth Lambton and he told me his views, but still he didn't appear to wish to talk. So I got on the problems of national defence which I had been studying and stated my opinions with a view to drawing him out. This had the desired effect and away he went. He said that unless we kept up the Navy to a two-power standard we were done. London would starve in a week

* Later 1st Lord Fisher of Kilverstone, Admiral of the Fleet. First Sea Lord, 1904–10 and 1914–15.

unless the seas were kept clear to bring in supplies. He sketched out what was later called 'the blue-water school'. I told him that I quite agreed with him but unless he had an Army at home large enough to prevent raids and make it necessary for a foreign enemy to land large numbers of men, the Navy would be useless. If 20,000 men could dodge the Fleet and land somewhere in England, they could march on London and create such a scare that we should be forced to capitulate without striking a blow. He was delighted with my arguments and got so excited talking that he had to stop and hold my arm to prevent my going on. He sketched out rather a wild scheme which was to reduce the Army and Navy to experts alone, and then keep a huge reserve of men who could become either soldiers or sailors. A beginning had been made in this direction by the nucleus crew system, but he wanted to carry the idea much further and make it apply to the Army. I told him that I very much doubted whether an Army composed of ninety per cent raw recruits would be any good, and I imagined that the highly trained German Army would soon make mincemeat of them, but he maintained that any idea of our fighting the Germans on land was absurd. By this scheme he would be able to reduce the income-tax by half, and that alone would be a blessing. We were out over two hours and when we returned he was still talking and holding me back from opening the door.

Personally I always had a great admiration for his genius and there seems no doubt that had it not been for the reforms which he pushed through in King Edward's reign, and which were resisted by the majority of naval officers, we should have come off second-best on the sea in our struggle with the Germans.

It was curious how he and Esher seemed to hit it off together, and I think the reason they got on so well was that they had the same type of mind. Both were very clever; both preferred to come in at the back door instead of the front; both had the early Italian type of mind. There was something tortuous about both of them, but while Fisher loved a fight and was prepared to stand or fall by his measures, Esher was very susceptible to public opinion and shrank from any responsibility. I always think that Esher's strong point was that he never minded who got credit for any measure he devised so long as it was adopted by the authorities.

Fisher was always very good company and loved telling naval yarns, which he did remarkably well. He had not, however, sufficient popularity or individuality to carry out his reforms single-handed, although he practically dominated every First Lord, no matter on which side of the House. It was King Edward's support that enabled him to carry out his reforms.

He very soon realized that if he was to retain King Edward's confidence he must make friends with the King's *entourage*, and he therefore with subtle flattery proceeded to make me one of his adherents. He would write me long letters apparently intended only for me as they were so outspoken, but really for King Edward to read. Unless he marked them private, which he rarely did, I always gave them to the King to read, and King Edward delighted in reading what he imagined was not intended for his eyes.

In April 1904 the King went down to stay with Jackie Fisher at Portsmouth. At that time the majority of the officers in the Navy were strongly opposed to Fisher's schemes while only a few of the cleverest officers supported him. The King, however, believed in Fisher and without quite understanding all the intricacies of the various questions involved, saw clearly that some reforms were needed. His Majesty consequently backed him while Charlie Beresford,* who hated Fisher and all his works, became the leader of the reactionary officers. These asserted that the reforms were quite unnecessary, that Fisher's methods were Machiavellian and un-English, and that Fisher had Malay blood in him; but as Fisher had the powerful backing of the King, these attacks proved harmless. Fisher always said that had it not been for King Edward's support he would never have succeeded in carrying out his various schemes. He always seemed to get the various First Lords of the Admiralty in his pocket, and Selborne, Cawdor, Tweedmouth and McKenna† went about repeating his cogent arguments, but they carried little or no weight with the officers of the Navy. His energy was marvellous, and although he had insisted on having no routine work when he became First Sea Lord, he used to get up at five o'clock every morning and do four hours' hard work before breakfast. He always said that these four hours of uninterrupted work were worth more than eight hours during the day. He interested and amused the King and often kept him up late at night propounding his theories of reform, and dilating upon

---

* Rear-Admiral Lord Charles Beresford, later 1st Lord Beresford and Admiral. After distinguished naval career became Conservative M.P. Brother of Lord Marcus Beresford.
† Successive First Lords of the Admiralty.

the virtues of his newest toy, the submarine. The King's wonderful gift of listening as if keenly interested, and his knowledge of human nature, were exemplified in a remarkable degree during this visit to Portsmouth. Fisher had explained the general principles on which the submarine worked and had outlined the various problems which had not yet been satisfactorily solved, so that the King knew a good deal before Captain Bacon, who later made a great name for himself* and became Admiral Sir Reginald Bacon, came to dinner, but he listened attentively to all Captain Bacon said when he practically repeated all that Fisher had told him. The following day we went on board a submarine and a very keen young officer showed us round. When he began at the beginning explaining things I felt inclined to say 'We know all about that', but the King listened attentively a third time to these explanations and asked several questions as if he were hearing about the submarine for the first time.

In 1907 Fisher sent me confidentially the draft of a memorandum which he had written on invasion for the Cabinet. I told him in my answer that a memorandum on such a subject without any mention of the Army, small as it was, would carry no conviction and I sketched out a short paragraph on the part the Army would have to play.

He replied: 'That codicil you propose is an excellent and valuable idea. *Bless you for telling me.*'

Later he wrote, 'Your words on the Army the most lucid and to the point ever yet written. Like Saul I don't believe you quite knew you were a prophet when you were prophesying. I am going to give them to the Prime Minister as they so exactly hit off the situation. I mean the following words: "In order to create a large reserve for great emergencies and in order to prevent a panic, it may be necessary to have a Territorial Army, but do it as cheaply as possible. My point is that if we are not safe from invasion then make us so. Spend money on submarines, etc., but don't waste money on an armed mob."' Naturally Fisher was delighted with this, but Haldane† on the other hand wrote a scathing minute on it because the Territorial Army was his creation.

Some time later Fisher wrote again: 'I sent your bit to the Prince of Wales and he is delighted with it. You will go down to posterity for

---

* As Commander of the Dover Patrol, 1915–18.
† Later 1st Viscount Haldane of Cloan. Secretary for War, 1905–12; Lord Chancellor, 1912–15 and 1924; Army reformer and philosopher.

that short paragraph – the best you ever wrote or can write. It's all in a nutshell. I call it the "Ponsonby Pill". It regularly clears them out and is damned hard and nasty to swallow.'

When McKenna became First Lord of the Admiralty Fisher was very much pressed by the Liberal Government to reduce the naval estimates, and to everyone's surprise he cut them down considerably. King Edward told me to write privately as from myself and enquire how it was that with former First Lords he had stoutly maintained that the millions he had asked for were the minimum he could accept, and yet here he was cheerfully acquiescing in a substantial reduction of the naval vote now that McKenna had become First Lord. I asked what new factor had made this reduction possible. This was a very awkward question, but he wrote at once, beginning 'My beloved Ponsonby. I call you beloved as you ask me a question which I just love answering.' He then wrote a long letter which, however, didn't answer my question at all.

Once an officer in India wrote to me and ended his letter 'Yours till Hell freezes'. I used this forcible expression in a letter to Fisher, and he adopted it instead of 'Yours sincerely' and used it a great deal.

In 1914, when he again began writing memoranda for the Cabinet, he sent me his drafts, but this was before he was brought back to the Admiralty during the War and he found that as a retired officer he didn't cut much ice. He wrote a sad PS to one letter: 'No chance of being anything now: let alone Viceroy of India. Another Pharaoh has arisen who knows not Joseph.'

The last time I saw him, towards the end of the War, he told me that the Labour party had asked him to be First Lord of the Admiralty if they came into office. I advised him not to go into politics at his age, but he never lived to have to make the decision.

In September 1907 I heard the other side of the controversy from Charlie Beresford when I stayed with the Londonderrys at Wynyard. One evening he gave me forty minutes' breezy conversation on the Navy, presumably hoping I should pass on to the King what he said. He always began by saying 'I wish to keep all argument impersonal', but after a short time he forgot and went on 'if it were not for that damned fellow Fisher'. The whole of his conversation was impreg-·nated with a hatred of Fisher, whom he accused of having poisoned him with the King. The chief points he made against the present adminstration were:

(1) That the firing which had attracted so much attention was really a farce. Fisher and Prince Louis of Battenberg had been duped by the Flag Captain, Mark Kerr,★ who had produced wonderful results under unfair conditions.

(2) The firing on the *Dreadnought* had been a farce and was laughed at by the Navy.

(3) The Home Fleet was a fraud and a deception. The ships were really a lot of lame ducks produced for effect.

(4) The nucleus crew system, although sound in theory, was really unworkable in practice and had really broken down owing to the details not being properly worked out.

(5) The whole Navy was dissatisfied, and until we had a real Board of the Admiralty we should never advance on sound principles. At present it was packed by Fisher.

Whenever I tried to bring him to the point by asking what he would do if he were to be appointed First Lord, he never seemed to have any satisfactory answer.

His last complaint was that there had been no cut-and-dried scheme of attack for the Channel Fleet; but this, as I told him, was really an attack on Wilson,† who commanded the Fleet before him.

I repeated all this to the King, who listened attentively but made no remark. He was so much in favour of Fisher that he didn't pay much attention to Beresford.

St John Brodrick was there, and I had some talk with him. He touched lightly on the difficulties he had had at the India Office, but we got on to Germany, and as he apparently had a great wish to talk on this subject, I did not attempt to turn the conversation back to India. He said that the King was always so busy and had so much to think about that he had never had a chance to tell His Majesty how much he deplored the strained relations with Germany. He laid great stress on the point that it was very necessary to find a successor to Sir Frank Lascelles from outside the Diplomatic Service. He said that all diplomatists were the same and followed the same groove. Unless someone was appointed who would help Englishmen to visit Berlin and *vice versa* we should never get on better terms with the Germans.

★   ★   ★

At Sandringham the King ordered a golf-links to be made in the Park:

★ Later Admiral Mark Kerr, Commander-in-Chief of the Adriatic Squadron, 1916–17; attempted the Atlantic flight, 1919.

† Admiral Sir Arthur Wilson preceded Beresford as Commander of the Channel Squadron.

48

the putting-greens were good though small and the fairways were properly mown, but there were no bunkers. To remedy this the agent, Mr Frank Beck, had placed wicker hurdles to indicate the places where the bunkers would eventually be dug. He argued that they could easily be moved to any position that the King eventually decided upon. This was perfectly sound in theory, but in practice it worked out very badly.

The first match we had on these links was the King and I playing the same ball against Seymour Fortescue. Nature had not made the King's figure suitable for driving a long ball, but he fancied himself at approaching and putting. Having blinked at the hurdles on the right and left of the fairway, the King proceeded to drive off and of course hit those on the right. The agent, who had come out to see whether the sites for the bunkers were right, looked horrified, but the King merely said, 'What a silly place to put a bunker! See that this is altered tomorrow; have them put much more to the right and further off the tee.'

Every other hole the same thing happened, and the King got louder and louder in his denunciation of the stupidity of the person who had placed the hurdles, while the agent took copious notes, but not being a golfer himself he had left the whole thing to the head gardener. However, as Seymour Fortescue kept on driving into the long grass we had quite a good game, and as the King did a very good approach shot at the eighth hole and sank a long putt at the ninth (we played only nine holes), we won on the last green and he quite recovered his temper.

The second day we played he took the even holes and of course drove into the hurdles again, when precisely the same thing happened and he ordered the hurdles to be moved. The third day was the most unnerving for the agent, because the hurdles at all the holes had been moved to different spots indicated by the King. The agent had taken the precaution of bringing out two men to move the hurdles anywhere. Again after viewing the hurdles distastefully the King never failed to drive into them and, in a voice of thunder, asked who had been stupid enough to place them there. When the agent replied by reading out his notes, which proved that it was the King himself who had selected the spot, the King exploded with rage and ordered all the hurdles to be taken away. This was done and orders were given to the head gardener to make proper bunkers. But unfortunately he knew little about this, and the following year erected only two

49

bunkers on the nine holes and made them like fortifications.

On one occasion I proposed to the King to get the professional over from Hunstanton to make a fourth, and I thought that he would be able to get the King over the ground. It was, however, not altogether a success to begin with, as the professional was so nervous that he made all sorts of bad strokes. He wanted to play the game of his life and developed a terrible hook on his drives. The King, who had to play the second shot out of a bush, or out of long grass, cursed him freely, which made him worse. Then he made a mess of his short game and couldn't putt at all, with the result that Seymour Fortescue and I won very easily.

On the way back to the house the King said that quite obviously the man was a very bad player and that no doubt I had selected him because I knew that I could beat him easily. As a matter of fact, the man could give me a stroke a hole any day.

I was so sorry for the professional that I sent him word that I would play him before breakfast the following morning. I explained to him that it was not necessary to play a super game. I had a handicap of nine and Fortescue of fifteen, so that all he had to do was to go straight and give the King a chance of doing well at the short game. The poor man was, however, still so nervous that he couldn't play at all the first three holes, but I got him to tell me some of his triumphs at golf, and he forgot his bad play with the King and settled down to his ordinary game. When the King came out to play at 11.30 he played beautifully and had quite got over his nervousness.

In the afternoon Queen Alexandra and I played against Princess Victoria and Francis Knollys. The Queen seemed to confuse it with hockey and was under the impression that one had to prevent the opponent putting the ball in the hole. This usually ended by a scrimmage on the green. She also thought that the person who got into the hole first won it, and asked me to hurry up and run between the strokes. It was very good fun, and we all laughed. Francis Knollys always played in a square-shaped billycock hat and a London tail coat, and hit so hard that his hat almost invariably fell off.

As golf proved so popular, the King gave orders that a golf course should be made at Windsor and wished it to be eighteen holes, but as we always took one and a half hours to do nine holes, I persuaded him to limit it to nine holes. I asked Mr Muir Fergusson, a distinguished amateur player who had laid out a course called New Zealand at Woking, to come down and sketch out the Windsor Castle links. He came down and took infinite trouble. We had men with stakes to mark the right and left of each bunker, and a man with a tape measure. Muir Fergusson succeeded in laying out nine good holes ending up just below the East Terrace, and I gave instructions to the farm bailiff to have the bunkers made.

I did not go to Windsor for two months as I presumed that a competent firm had been employed, but I suddenly received an irate telegraph from the King to the effect that the private park at Windsor had been ruined and that I was to order the bunkers to be razed to the ground. When I went to Windsor I was aghast at what I saw. The man who had undertaken to make the bunkers had obviously no knowledge of golf grounds and didn't know the ABC of the business. At each post which had been driven into the ground to make the right and left of the bunkers he had erected a mound four feet high and a ditch four feet deep but only ten yards long. The result was that the ground looked like a graveyard with tombstones dotted about. I was furious and went in search of the man. I found him talking to the farm bailiff. He said that he proposed to make the last bunker in the shape of a Victoria Cross with flowers! I told him what I thought of him and said it was criminal of him to undertake a job like this when he had not the most elementary knowledge of bunkers. I gave orders that he and his men were to leave the ground at once,, and I told the farm bailiff to see that they never returned. We had a breezy five minutes, and I closed the discussion by saying that unless he and his men cleared out in an hour I would instruct the police to push them out. I gave orders that the bunkers were to be razed to the ground, and sent for the professional from the Datchet links close by and explained to him how the bunkers should go, asking him to superintend the work. Eventually this came out all right and Muir Fergusson came down and made a few alterations. He was a big red-faced man and probably accustomed to have his way, but when the King happened to come along he became tongue-tied. It was unfortunate that I did not have an opportunity of explaining what a swell he was in the golfing world because the King thought he was a professional. However, when I explained everything afterwards to the King he sent him a cigarette-case with the Royal cypher on it.

Other leading golfers were invited to play with the King. First of all Kirkaldy came down from Scotland, but he got rather drunk and was sent back. Then Ben Sayers came and was a great success. He was always anxious to praise the King's shots and once when the King topped his drive, he exclaimed, 'Very good direction, Your Majesty.' Once when the King said he would play at three o'clock Sayers teed up two new balls ready but received a message that the King would not play till four, so he went away. Meanwhile Queen Alexandra came out to play and, finding two new balls, played a sort of hockey with them till they were battered into a three-cornered shape. She then replaced the balls on the tee and went in. At four the King came out and asked Sayers if he had got any golf balls. He replied that they were ready on the tee, but when the King saw them he thought Sayers was trying to be funny. Luckily Sayers had plenty more, but it was not till tea-time that the King learnt that the Queen and Princess Victoria had played golf at three, and grasped why the balls were so battered.

★   ★   ★

It was not till the middle of July that I received a message from the King that I was to go with him on board the *Victoria & Albert* where he would convalesce after his operation. I travelled down with Harry Legge and Harry Stonor★ in the same train as the King and Queen. The King was carried to the train on a stretcher, and we went down to Portsmouth at a slow pace. When we arrived the King was carried on board the yacht by bluejackets. The deck cabin where we usually sat or played bridge had been fitted up as a sick-room with a bed in the middle and tables with bottles of medicine and dressings.

We went in to luncheon, but of course the King did not come. To me it was like a fairy-tale, coming after South Africa, where I had become accustomed to bully beef and other tinned foods. Moreover, after having come to the conclusion that my position was very precarious and that I should soon have to find some other job, it was astonishing to find myself not only 'in waiting' but again as Acting Private Secretary.

At the luncheon table there were gold cups and masses of roses. The Queen sat at the end of the table and rang a tinkly bell when the servants were wanted. The Marine band under Lieutenant Miller played soft music outside on the deck. I sat between Princess Maud, later Queen of Norway, and Sir Frederick Treves, the great surgeon, a man with a keen sense of humour but a certain contempt for the

★ Later Sir Harry Stonor, Gentleman-Usher and Groom-in-Waiting to King Edward and King George V.

human race. After luncheon the King sent for me and I found him in a blue flannel suit lying on the bed puffing a cigar. He greeted me with 'Hallo, Fritz. I little thought the last time I saw you that I should be like this now.' He added, 'You can't think what a pleasure it is to get out of my sick-room at Buckingham Palace.' I asked him if he had suffered much pain and he said that at first it had been very painful but he hoped that was all over now. The Queen then came in and talked away for a few minutes to me, but I felt I ought to make myself scarce, and when Caesar, the King's terrier, was brought in, I discreetly left.

The King began doing a little business and sent for me twice a day to give me letters to answer, but I soon saw that no one was sending him any difficult stuff. He was still in bed or else lying on the bed, but able to write. It seemed a great pleasure to him to be able to make a start.

After dinner the Queen took me down and showed me her cabin, which was lovely and not in the least like a cabin but more like a drawing-room. It was painted white and panelled with bookcases, with a boudoir grand piano and very comfortable armchairs around what looked like a fireplace. She was in great form and full of jokes. She showed me with pride her bookplate which she had designed herself. On it there were her favourite books, her favourite music, her favourite dogs, a picture of Windsor, a picture of the Palace at Copenhagen, and a little strip of music, the first bars of her favourite song; a most elaborate bookplate, and she said she had been told it would be quite impossible to have so many different things portrayed, yet there it was.

Divine Service on board was an interesting sight as all the yacht's crew attended and sang lustily while the Marine band played. Hedworth Lambton, the Commodore, officiated, but naturally refused to intone, and read the service and responses like short snappy words of command while the band and two hundred men responded with full choral effect. The Queen, Princess Victoria, and Princess Maud with the members of the Household sat facing the yacht's crew, and the King had his bed wheeled up to the window of his deck cabin and looked on benignly.

The Queen, accompanied by Treves and myself, paid a surprise visit to Netley Hospital. We went in a steam pinnace and, although the doctors and nurses were in the secret, the patients had no idea who she was. She was delighted when she asked one of the men whether he was better and he replied, 'Yes, Miss.' It was, however, unlikely that none of the men should recognize her and soon all those who were able to walk came crowding round, and we had some difficulty in restraining them. One man lying down with his head all bandaged up attracted the Queen's attention and she asked him about South Africa. He replied he had been out at the war for two and a half years and had taken part in almost every big battle. The Queen asked him at what battle he had been wounded and he replied that he had never been wounded at all but that on arrival at Southampton, he had slipped and fallen down the hatchway!

★   ★   ★

The Shah of Persia★ had intended to pay an official visit to the King, but this was postponed owing to the Coronation being delayed. All that could therefore be arranged was a visit to the King on board the yacht on August 20, and with this the Shah was satisfied. He wanted the Order of the Garter, and he did not mind much whether it was given to him in London or on the yacht.

Francis Knollys had given me no papers on the subject: in fact I didn't know that there had been any correspondence about this between Lord Lansdowne, who was Secretary of State for Foreign Affairs, and the King. He left me to deal with this most explosive material as best I could.

When the visit was first arranged the Shah had made it clear that he expected to be given the Garter and that he would accept no other Order. Originally the Garter was only given to Christian Sovereigns and infidels were not considered eligible; but Queen Victoria had made exceptions in the cases of the two Sultans of Turkey when they came to England, and had also given it to the Shah's father, and this had created an awkward precedent. When Lansdowne found that the Shah would not be content with anything but the Garter, he asked the King to make another exception and give that Order in this case. Here there was a misunderstanding: Lansdowne understood from the King that he approved of the Garter being given while the King maintained that he had never agreed. It was a pity that there was nothing on paper because in a discussion a wrong impression may so easily have been given.

★ Muzaffar-ad-Din; succeeded Nasir-ad-Din, who had been assassinated in 1896; succeeded in 1906 by Mohammed Ali, who was deposed in 1909.

Lansdowne, under the impression that the King approved, let it be understood by the Persian Minister that the Garter would be given, but as one of the non-Christian Sovereigns had raised an objection to the star of the Garter having a Christian emblem – the Cross – he hit upon the idea of having a special star made without the Cross of St George and sent the design down for the King to see.

Such was the position when I was brought into the dispute. A Foreign Office box came down looking harmless enough, but when the King opened it, read Lansdowne's letter and saw the design, there was an explosion. He was so angry that he flung the design across his cabin and it went through the porthole and, as I thought, into the sea. Later, however, I found that it had fallen into a steam pinnace and had been brought back by the stoker, who presumed it was a picture of some value. Of course this was all Greek to me and I was at first totally unable to understand why the King was so angry. He dictated some very violent remarks for me to incorporate in my letter to Lansdowne. From these and from further conversation on the subject I grasped that it was a serious matter. I therefore suggested to the King that I should write to Knollys and ask him to convey His Majesty's wishes to Lansdowne, but this proved impossible as Knollys had already gone up to Balmoral. I therefore wrote a bowdlerized version of the King's withering remarks and pointed out that His Majesty had never approved of the Shah being given the Garter. If this Order was to be given to non-Christian Sovereigns, surely the Emperor of Japan should be the first to receive it, but once this was begun we should have to consider all sorts of Eastern potentates. I added that the King had been shocked at the proposal to omit the Cross of St George and wouldn't hear of such a proposal.

Lansdowne replied that the mistake was entirely his and that he must have misunderstood what the King said, but as he had, in his capacity as Minister for Foreign Affairs, said that the Shah would be given the Garter, there was no alternative for him but to place his resignation in the King's hands. He then appears to have laid the whole matter before Arthur Balfour, the Prime Minister, who took the view that as he had, rightly or wrongly, as Minister of Foreign Affairs, practically promised the Garter, he must of course be supported, but the proposal to eliminate the Cross of St George was fantastic.

Lansdowne then came down to see the King on board the Royal yacht and His Majesty promised to reconsider the matter carefully.

Eventually the King agreed with Arthur Balfour and so the trouble subsided; but relations between the King and Lansdowne, which had never been good, deteriorated still further.

The Shah brought down a large suite and there was not sufficient room for them in the dining saloon. The King therefore arranged that I should take half of them to luncheon on board the *Osborne*, the second of the Royal yachts. When, however, I tried to do so, they flatly refused to come and sat down and sulked. They thought they had been insulted and all sat together whispering. I didn't know enough of the Eastern mind to be able to handle them. I addressed them slowly so that they would understand and told them that unless they came with me on board the *Osborne* they would get no luncheon. I added that in any case they could not sit where they were as the King and Queen and the Shah would want those chairs after luncheon, but I would come back in five minutes to conduct them to their luncheon. When I did so they rose reluctantly, and with some more coaxing I induced them to come with me. The officers of the *Osborne* were drawn up to receive them and played up well, making much of them.

★   ★   ★

The King at once took strong measures to stop the drinking that went on, but, I think wisely, did not try to stop it altogether. In Queen Victoria's reign whenever anyone went out stalking, a whole bottle of whisky was given out, and whatever the guest did not drink became the perquisite of the stalker. It was quite a common thing for a stalker to come to the castle and drink off a glass of neat whisky before he started. Of course if he went out stalking no harm was done, but when the weather was impossible and the mist came down he retired to his house and started the day slightly intoxicated. The amount of whisky consumed by the servants was truly stupendous. Whenever the Queen went out driving, a bottle of whisky was put under the coachman's seat and was supposed to provide stimulant to anyone who had had an accident. It was said that early in the Queen's reign a poor man had been found at the side of the road in a state of exhaustion and that Her Majesty had remarked what a pity it was that no one had any stimulant to revive him. This was at once rectified and innumerable bottles of whisky must have gone astray in this way. But the whole atmosphere was wrong. A drunken man was so common that no one ever remarked on it. Before my day there were what were called 'larders'. The stags that had been shot during the day were taken from the larders and placed in a row and all the gillies carried torches. The Queen came out after dinner and dancing took place, all of which was very pretty, but after she left it became an orgy of drink.

Another occasion when whisky was freely given was the anniversary of the Prince Consort's birthday. All the stalkers, gillies and people on the estate were expected to attend dressed in top-hats (what the people called a funeral hat) and black coats. A prayer was said in front of the Prince Consort's statue, and the Queen drove there in her carriage with two grey horses and an outrider. Then whisky was sent out as light refreshment at the back of the wood. The result was that the whole community was three parts intoxicated and when we went for a walk in the afternoon it was no uncommon sight to find a man in a top-hat and frock-coat fast asleep in the woods. Sir James Reid, the doctor, helped the King, as he knew the men so well that he could do almost anything with them.

All this was now altered, and although a flask of whisky was provided with the luncheon for anyone going out stalking, bottles were no longer the perquisite of the stalker.

The King therefore, without overdoing it, took steps to stop the unfortunate amount of drinking that used to take place formerly, but the regulations he made were enforced with the utmost severity. I was really very sorry for one of the stalkers, a splendid-looking man with a white beard, of the name of Cameron. A deer drive was ordered and all the stalkers and gillies turned out, but the weather made everything impossible, for not only were there sheets of rain, but the mist was so low on the hills that no one could see anything, so the deer drive was cancelled. No sooner had all the men been sent back to their houses than the sun came out and it cleared up completely. The King therefore said he would have luncheon out on the hill and the deer drive would take place afterwards. Cameron, who lived some way off, feeling sure that he would not be wanted, had commenced drinking, when a messenger arrived summoning him. Had it been later in the day he would have been too drunk to obey the summons, but as it was he was only rather drunk. He turned up for luncheon and instead of keeping out of the light he insisted of going up to the King and talking. Of course His Majesty saw he was drunk although he could just walk. The King called up the head stalker and told him that Cameron was drunk and that he was to be dismissed at once, and dismissed he was, without a pension. This was making an example with a vengeance, and it was said that the stalkers and gillies were partly resentful at a man with thirty years' service being sacked, and partly frightened lest the same thing should happen to them. Cameron, who hailed from Inverness-shire, returned to his birthplace a broken man, but the King told me confidentially that when the affair had blown over he would see that Cameron was given a pension on the understanding that he did not return to Balmoral.

In December the King and Queen went to stay at Gopsall with Lord★ and Lady Howe and took with them Lady Emily Kingscote, Harry Legge and myself. By this time the arrangement whereby I should do alternate months with Arthur Davidson was in full swing and it worked very well. We worked in together keeping each other informed of all that went on during our month's waiting, with copies of all the correspondence that took place.

At Gopsall there was a large party, but George Howe most kindly asked either Harry Legge or me to shoot every day. It was all very well done and the house had just been done up with bathrooms galore and everything most comfortable. About the fourth night I sat next to Lady de Grey, who sat by the King, and she whispered to me, 'For Heaven's sake suggest a topic for me to discuss with the King as I have sat next to him for three nights.' I replied, 'Give away your relations and friends and repeat any secrets about them.' She laughed and said, 'But I did that the first night!'

The King undoubtedly liked masses of pheasants driven over his head about the height of an ordinary tree, but while most people would get rattled at the number he slowly selected one and shot it, generally behind him. He was quite good at shooting with a crowd looking on, as he never seemed to miss; but then he never fired at a difficult bird.

At Christmas-time I went to Sandringham, where I found that the festivities began on Christmas Eve. The King and Queen did the presents themselves and spent hours in the ballroom arranging everything. In the centre of the ballroom was a large Christmas-tree and round this were arranged trestle tables the whole length of the room, covered with a white tablecloth. Every member of the party had a bit of these tables portioned off to them, and the clergy, doctors, etc., also came and had their share. It was all beautifully done, and the pleasure of giving seemed never to leave their Majesties, as it so often

★ Richard Penn Curzon, 4th Earl Howe; Lord-in-Waiting, 1900–03.

does with rich people. Before dinner on Christmas Eve we all assembled in the corridor outside the ballroom and one by one we were called in. It was always a rather trying experience as one found the King on one side and the Queen on the other explaining who gave what present and giving particulars about the various articles. One stood gasping one's thanks to each alternately, and it was always a relief when the next person was called in. It was impossible to make a set speech, and most people, including myself, continued gasping 'Thank you so much'.

I was quite overcome at first by the number of presents I received. There were prints, water-colours, silver cigarette-cases, a silver inkstand, pins, studs and several books. Gottlieb's band played in the gallery, and every evening after dinner we went to the ballroom and looked at everyone else's presents. The King and Queen, of course, received wonderful things from their relations in Europe, the Emperor of Russia sending particularly lovely things by special messenger.

On New Year's Eve all the presents were taken away and the tables were arranged differently and closer to the Christmas-tree. All the servants and workers on the estate came in and remained outside the row of tables while the presents were massed round the Christmas-tree. Each servant and employee drew two numbers on entering the room, and the Princesses and members of the Household took the numbers and found the present. Of course often a present didn't fit the recipient and a housemaid might get a razor and a footman a powder-puff, but these could be exchanged later. Some eight hundred presents were given in this way and it seemed to give much pleasure. At the conclusion the Christmas-tree was stripped and all the toys and sweets were given to the children.

★   ★   ★

King Edward had always been a lover of European travel, but as Prince of Wales his various visits to European capitals or spas were strictly unofficial. Shortly after his accession to the throne, however, he determined to make a Mediterranean tour which should include several official visits. Whether he anticipated opposition on the part of the Government to these official foreign visits I never knew, but the arrangements which he made for his tour early in 1903 were kept a dead secret and most of the suite had no idea where they were going.

The King kept the whole arrangements in his own hands and knew that he could rely on the discretion of the various members of his Household to keep everything as quiet as possible. Everything was in water-tight compartments, so that the person who was responsible for the orders to be given to the yacht knew nothing about the telegrams and letters that were being sent to foreign capitals. Beyond the fact that I was to form one of the suite, I knew nothing at all about the arrangements.

The suite consisted of the Hon. Charles Hardinge,★ Minister Plenipotentiary and Assistant Under-Secretary for Foreign Affairs; Major-General Sir Stanley Clarke, Acting Master of the Household; Rear-Admiral the Hon. Hedworth Lambton, Equerry and in command of the Royal yacht; Captain the Hon. Seymour Fortescue, Equerry; Sir Francis Laking, the King's physician; Chevalier de Martino, the marine painter; and myself as Equerry and Acting Private Secretary. The Marquis de Soveral, the Portuguese Ambassador, came as far as Lisbon, which was to be our first port of call.

In Queen Victoria's reign it was the custom for a Cabinet Minister to accompany the Sovereign, but King Edward made a new departure in taking with him a comparatively unknown Secretary from the Diplomatic Service. At first it was said that Hardinge had been selected because he had married one of Queen Alexandra's Ladies-in-Waiting, but this was quite wrong. King Edward had with unerring judgement discovered Hardinge as the rising man in diplomacy, and thought he would be far more useful than a Cabinet Minister, who would probably be unable to talk French or German. It was certainly a very happy selection, for Hardinge proved to be a man of exceptional ability.

The decision to take three Equerries, and make one do the work of the Master of the Household, never seemed quite a success as the duties of the latter practically ceased when we landed, but everything went smoothly and there was rarely any difficulty. I am sure it was the King's original intention to leave Martino on the yacht, but with that kindness of heart which characterized all his actions, he ended by allowing Martino to accompany him. Anybody more inappropriate in the suite of an English King than an Italian painter it is impossible to

★ Later 1st Baron Hardinge of Penshurst. Assistant Under-Secretary of State for Foreign Affairs, 1903–04; Permanent Under-Secretary of State for Foreign Affairs, 1906–10 and 1916–20; Ambassador to Russia, 1904–06; Viceroy of India, 1910–16; Ambassador to France, 1920–22.

imagine. First of all Martino objected to ranking last in the suite, and King Edward told me to bring him the list so that he might decide what should be done about this. I told him that I had no objection to ranking last and possibly Martino would be satisfied if he was placed above me, but complications followed because Seymour Fortescue, hearing of this ridiculous protest on Martino's part, also offered to rank last. Then Hedworth Lambton, the Commodore of the Royal yachts, had to be placed among the suite, and on hearing about Martino also asked to be placed last. This amused the King very much, but he definitely decided that Martino should rank just above me to satisfy him, and that the others should be placed in their proper order.

We arrived at Lisbon on April 3rd, and as soon as we dropped anchor the Embassy staff came on board. The King of Portugal came later in a green and gold barge rowed by eighty men in red. It was just like the Middle Ages, for these barges had been used for centuries.

King Edward was dressed as Colonel of a Portuguese cavalry regiment, a uniform that certainly was not becoming to a stout man as the coat was very short and showed an immense expanse of breeches. The King of Portugal welcomed His Majesty effusively and then both Kings presented their suites by name. We were all new at the game at that time, and did not know we had to be presented, so that the King found us scattered all over the yacht when he wanted to present us.

In the evening we went ashore in three picturesque barges while bands played, guns boomed, and spasmodic cheering was heard on shore. The municipal magnates were drawn up on the quay and an address of welcome was read in Portuguese, to which the King replied in English. We were then all conducted to gilded coaches amidst more cheering. These coaches were not unlike the one that Cinderella had, to take her to the ball, with exquisitely painted panels in the style of Boucher, but they were so old and cracked that I feared lest the floor-boards of the one in which Martino and I drove should give way and we should have to run inside the coach. The first four coaches were each drawn by six white Arab ponies and the last two by black English horses, while a large body of cavalry formed the escort. The drive through the streets of Lisbon lasted an hour and a half, and everywhere there were dense crowds.

On arrival at the Palace the King was received by the Queen Mother, Maria Pia, in the absence of the Queen of Portugal, and we were shown to our rooms. I had a suite of rooms given to me which were magnificently ugly, but not comfortable as we understand comfort. There was a musty smell about the room which gave me the impression that they had not been used for years, although bathrooms had been specially installed for our ablutions. My sitting-room was quite medieval, having heavy red velvet curtains, not only on the windows but also over the doors, old-fashioned massive furniture and huge pictures, while the bedroom contained a four-poster bed with heavy curtains. Soveral had obviously written to ask that every effort should be made to provide us with English luxuries, for whisky and soda was placed in our rooms at night and a cup of tea was brought us in the morning.

The following day the two Kings went to Cintra for luncheon and returned in the afternoon, when the King received the Corps Diplomatique. This was one of the most trying ceremonies a Sovereign had to undertake, for the Ambassadors and Ministers, supported by their staffs, were drawn up round the room and the King had to speak to each one and never seemed to find any difficulty in doing it quite naturally. His method was to talk to A and then draw B into the conversation, move on imperceptibly and while apparently listening to B, draw C into conversation, and so on, but it required a very alert mind not to make a mistake and to recognize each country by the uniform and decorations so that the Peruvian was not mistaken for the Bulgarian Minister.

The next day, April 4th, was one of the most tiring I have ever spent in my life, for I had to stand practically the whole day. In the morning the King received addresses at the museum of the Geographical Society and we all stood behind him on a platform. After luncheon we went to see pigeon-shooting in the gardens of the Ajuda which lasted from two to five. According to the etiquette, no one was allowed to sit except the two Kings, and we had to stand in an enclosure in the hot sun, bored to death with the competition. The King of Portugal was most anxious to win but only got third prize although he was a wonderful shot. At five we went to tea with the Queen Mother, but there again it was contrary to etiquette to sit and we had therefore to stand for an hour. We got back to our rooms soon after six, but as the banquet in full uniform took place at 6.30, we only just had time to dress.

There were a hundred people at the banquet, and it seemed very well done, but we had hardly time to drink our coffee before we were hurried off to a gala performance at the Opera. The Royal Box was in the centre of the house, and contained only three huge gilt chairs for the two Kings and the Queen Mother, and I could hardly believe my ears when I was told that according to the etiquette we all had to stand throughout the performance. I had already stood about for four hours in the afternoon and an hour in the morning, and I was expected to enjoy the performance dolled up in uniform and standing to attention. I stood it for an hour and twenty minutes and then I told Hedworth Lambton that I really could not stand any more and he agreed to retire quietly from the box and go and sit down outside somewhere, but when we tried to slip out quickly, the Portuguese thought we were being polite and were putting them in front of us. They said 'Please, please', and insisted on our remaining in the front row. We were so much taller than the Portuguese that it was impossible to escape detection. At the end of a scene there was frantic applause and bouquets were passed up to the prima donna, which gave us the opportunity of gliding back and then leaving the box. When we got out into the corridor there were no chairs or seats of any description, but on peering about I found two in the ladies' cloak-room and there we sat and smoked cigarettes, though not for long, for an aristocratic-looking female appeared at the door and not unnaturally resented our presence. She went off to find someone to turn us out and soon the corridor was full of irate women. So we thought it wise to beat a retreat, but nothing would induce me to return to the box, and after sauntering about we found a bench in the foyer and there we sat till we thought the performance was nearly over, when we mixed with the crowd of officials in the Royal Box, and this time when they said 'Please, please', we allowed ourselves to be pushed again into the front row.

An awkward thing happened to me on Sunday the 5th. Sotheby, one of the Privy Purse clerks, who was with me as typist and secretary, asked for leave to go out with one of the attaches at the British Legation. I at once gave him leave as I could not imagine that anything would be wanted on a Sunday, but all of a sudden after he had left the King told me that he was going to Cascaes, and as a purely formal business the Mayor of that place intended to hand an address which would not be read and a typed reply would be all that was necessary. I went to Sotheby's room and found everything carefully locked up. I wanted some paper with the Royal Arms on it and his typewriter, but all his boxes were locked. I had therefore to break the padlock on his typewriter and prise open his stationery box, all of which took some time, but I managed to produce some non-committal reply with commonplace remarks for the King to hand to the Mayor.

One afternoon we went for a motor drive round the outskirts of Lisbon, and Hedworth Lambton and I went in a car driven by the Duc d'Oporto, the King of Portugal's brother, who was a most frightening driver and who insisted on playing practical jokes. These so unnerved Lambton, who said he didn't think it funny to have his neck broken for a joke, that he insisted on getting into another car the first time he stopped. I was unfortunately seated by the Duke and I came to the conclusion that while he might possibly kill someone on the road, there was little danger of anything happening to him or to me. As we drove home he asked whether I would like to see him put the cars behind us in the ditch, and I nervously replied that I did not understand what he meant. 'You will see,' he replied, and looking back he waved them to come on, at the same time quickening his pace till he must have been going about fifty miles an hour. We arrived suddenly at a T-shaped cross-roads and he put the brakes on so suddenly that I was nearly shot out of the car, but by this means he was just able to turn sharp to the left. The cars behind being quite unprepared had no chance and two of them got into a ditch, which was luckily not very deep, whilst a third skidded into a wall, all of which seemed to amuse him immensely. Another time he pretended to run straight into the crowd and then jammed on the brakes so that the car stopped suddenly within a few feet of them. The crowd rushed away in confusion, men, women, and children tripping and falling over one another in every direction. This made him laugh heartily, while I sat with my hair standing erect on my head. He ended up by careering over a drawbridge, through an archway and into a courtyard, only missing the wall by an inch, and I made a mental resolution never to drive with him again.

★   ★   ★

We had some difficulty over the King's wish to visit the Pope.★ He said that among his subjects were millions of Roman Catholics and that they would be inclined to take offence if he took no notice of the Pope when he was in Rome. There was no doubt he firmly intended

★ Leo XIII.

64

to pay this visit and the Cabinet in London had been told that such was His Majesty's intention. Had it been left at that there would have been no difficulty, but unfortunately the King sent another telegram asking their advice, and Arthur Balfour, the Prime Minister, found himself in an awkward position. If he advised and approved of the King visiting the Pope, he stood to be shot at by members of Parliament and religious bodies, but if on the other hand he officially told the King not to go, it looked petty and small-minded. When Hardinge's second telegram was read before the Cabinet they came to the conclusion that as their advice had been asked they could not be expected to sanction such a visit, and they therefore said that they adhered to their original decision and thought it most inadvisable that His Majesty, who was a Protestant, should see the Pope. When the King received a long cypher telegram to this effect, he was perfectly furious and dictated to Hardinge a strongly worded message, such a message as would have put the backs up not only of the Cabinet but the two Houses of Parliament. Hardinge, who at that time did not know the King's ways and did not understand that messages of this sort had to be toned down, wrote it out practically verbatim and asked me to cypher it to the Prime Minister. As I read it I felt instinctively that if this message was sent there would be no alternative for Arthur Balfour but to send in his resignation, and after reading it several times I came to the conclusion that it was impossible to send such a plain-spoken provocative message as it was. I perfectly understood that the King wished to see the Pope, but this message could have but one result, and so far from furthering the King's wishes, the Prime Minister would probably send a reply which would make the visit impossible.

My difficulty was that everyone had gone on shore to an official dinner and I was left alone on board as I had so much to do. It would have been a comparatively simple matter had I been able to go to the King and show him the draft of an amended message or even to consult Hardinge, but every moment was precious and they might not return till midnight. I determined to rewrite the message on my own responsibility and send it off. It was a telegram from the King and not from Hardinge, and I felt that I should not risk getting Hardinge into trouble. I therefore altered the whole telegram and in conciliatory language said that the King quite realized the difficulties of the Cabinet and that he did not wish to put them in a false position. He would take the initiative himself and if he found that circumstances rendered it advisable that he should pay a visit to the Pope, he would do so

65

without consulting them and entirely on his own responsibility. They must, however, leave it to him to decide. The gist of the message was that he withdrew his former request for advice and would act on his own responsibility. This telegram I sent off at once in cypher. When everyone returned on board about midnight, I thought I ought to tell Hardinge what I had done and showed him a copy of what I had sent. He was extremely angry. He said I had no right to alter the King's words. He accused me of putting him in a false position and said it was an unheard-of thing to tamper with a message from the King to the Prime Minister. We had a heated discussion on the subject and I replied that all I had done was to further the King's wishes. Had the message been sent as he had written it, the visit would have been out of the question. The Cabinet had but to publish the telegrams and the whole of the British nation would be on their side. I maintained that it was my duty as Private Secretary to do all I could to help the King to carry out his intention to visit the Pope and that therefore I was right in altering the telegram. The King often dictated telegrams couched in too forcible language, and, as he never found any difficulty in expressing himself, he rattled them off and it was my duty to see there was nothing in them that would give offence.

Hardinge, however, was not appeased and pointed out with some truth that in this case it had not been a matter of softening the language used. I had, he said, altered the message and given it quite a different interpretation. If things went wrong, as he feared they would, he would have no alternative but to send in his resignation. I replied that he was blameless and that he was at perfect liberty to throw the blame on me.

He was so much put out at this that instead of going to bed he continued to pace the deck for some time meditating what he ought to do. Finally about one o'clock he came down to my cabin where I was still writing and said he would await Arthur Balfour's reply before coming to any decision.

The next morning came a long cypher telegram from Arthur Balfour and I nervously decyphered it. It was a great relief to me to find that what I had predicted had come true. Balfour at once accepted the situation and said he had explained the whole matter to the Cabinet, who were quite willing to withdraw their advice and who quite agreed that it was best to leave the matter in the King's hands. This was a great triumph for me, and I took it at once to Hardinge, who most generously agreed that I had done the right thing.

Later I explained to the King that I had altered his message as I feared that it might put up the backs of the Cabinet and that they would feel it their duty to protest, which might make a visit to the Pope difficult if not impossible. As Balfour's answer had been just what the King wanted, he said he thought I was quite right.

★   ★   ★

On May 1st we left Rome amidst great enthusiasm and travelled to Paris. I tried to find out who was in favour of this visit. Sir Edmund Monson, the British Ambassador in Paris, as he told me later, was certainly not. Lord Lansdowne and the Foreign Office very much doubted the wisdom of a visit in view of the hostile attitude of the Parisian crowd towards England. Arthur Balfour and the Cabinet didn't quite know enough about it to be able to express any opinion on the subject, but as apparently they were not consulted they were quite content to let the King do as he liked. Hardinge told me it was entirely the King's idea and while no one was in favour of the visit, the Government hardly had sufficient grounds for actually opposing it.

At Dijon the Ambassador, Sir Edmund Monson, joined the train together with the French officers attached to the King during the visit. This necessitated our making conversation to them all the way to Paris, but they were all charming and easy to talk to. We arrived at the station in the Bois de Boulogne, where we found President Loubet and a large number of officials. We drove in six carriages each drawn by four horses with postilions, and were escorted by a large number of French cavalry. There was an immense crowd in the streets and all along the Champs-Elysées. Whether the King had a good reception or not I didn't know, but I was told afterwards that the cheers were mostly for the President. As regards myself in the last carriage I received anything but a pleasant ovation, for the cheers had become jeers by the time I came, and being in a red coat I was selected by the crowd for witticisms. There were cries of 'Vive Marchand!' and 'Vive Fashoda!', 'Vivent les Boers!', and occasionally 'Vive Jeanne d'Arc!', which seemed to be going back a long way in history. On one or two occasions a voice shouted quite a long sentence which I was unable to catch, and the crowd was convulsed with laughter, all of which showed that we were anything but popular in Paris.

At the British Embassy we were not very comfortable, as the Monsons only lived in certain rooms and usually left the main apartments, except the drawing-rooms, empty of furniture. The 'Garde-meuble', where all the best furniture from the old palaces was stored, sent some lovely bits of furniture and these empty rooms were luxuriously furnished. Half an hour after we arrived we had to get into carriages again and pay a formal visit to Monsieur and Madame Loubet. The first speech the King made was to the British Chamber of Commerce and this made a great impression on the French mind when it was translated and published the next day. In the evening we went to the Théâtre Français where we saw *L'Autre Danger*. During the *entr'acte* the King insisted on walking about in the crowd in the foyer, much to the terror of the police.

The following day we had a long drive down to Vincennes, where eighteen thousand men marched past. We drove through the poorer parts of Paris and although the crowd were not very enthusiastic there were no rude remarks.

It was at the Hôtel de Ville that the King made a short speech which entirely changed the whole atmosphere and brought all the French round at once. The actual speech in all its brevity was as follows:

'Je désire vous exprimer combien je suis vivement touché de vos bonnes paroles. Il aurait été fâcheux, en passant par votre belle ville, de ne pouvoir m'arrêter à l'Hôtel de Ville. Bien sincèrement, je vous remercie de l'accueil que vous m'avez fait aujourd'hui.

'Je n'oublierai jamais ma visite à votre charmante ville, et je puis vous assurer que c'est avec le plus grand plaisir que je reviens à Paris, où je me trouve toujours comme si j'étais chez moi.'

That last phrase went home, and as he sat down he received a tremendous ovation. He seemed to have captured Paris by storm. From that moment everything was changed wherever we went. Not only the King but all of the suite were received with loud and repeated cheering. It was the most marvellous transformation, and all in three days. The first day distinctly antagonistic, the second cold, and finally frenzied enthusiasm.

In the evening there was a State banquet at the Palace of the Elysée to which 130 people were invited. I was amused to see that although France was a republic, everything was done in exactly the same way as in monarchical countries. There were hundreds of footmen with powdered hair, and the whole banquet was precisely the same as we had had in Rome and Lisbon, the only difference being Monsieur and Madame Loubet instead of a King and Queen. At the conclusion of dinner the President proposed the King's health in a speech prepared by the Protocole. He was obviously nervous and had pinned the speech to one of the candlesticks in front of him, which necessitated his leaning forward to read it. The result was that only a certain number of people near him could hear what he said. When he had finished, the King got up and replied in French. He never seemed at a loss for a word and without any notes or paper in his hand he made an admirable speech, speaking like a Frenchman, which captivated all the guests. They had been accustomed to hear a President mumbling a speech and they were carried away with enthusiasm. The King spoke clearly and distinctly so that all the people at the further ends of a long table were able to hear, and this no doubt accounted for the enthusiastic ovation he received when he sat down. There are very few people who can make a telling speech in a foreign language, but His Majesty was able to do this both in French and German. On the 4th we left and returned to London.

The visit eventually had far-reaching effects, and it was all very well for Lord Lansdowne to claim afterwards the credit for the *Entente Cordiale*, but neither he nor the Government could have got the French people round from hostility to enthusiastic friendship in the way King Edward did. As M. Paul Cambon, the French Ambassador in London, remarked, any clerk at the Foreign Office could draw up a treaty, but there was no one else who could have succeeded in producing the right atmosphere for a *rapprochement* with France. After the banquet the King cleverly singled out Prince Radolin, the German Ambassador, to talk to, obviously with a view to smoothing the ruffled feelings of Germany.

The visit to Paris always seemed to me to strain the limitations of a constitutional monarch to breaking point. The King went to Paris with no Cabinet Minister to advise him or to act as a liaison between him and the Government, and yet he reversed the whole policy of this country.

The idea of an *entente* with France was by no means new. In 1891 Chamberlain met Clemenceau in London and discussed the possibilities of France and England coming to some arrangement, but partly because they could not agree and partly because Salisbury refused to budge from his policy of splendid isolation the whole thing ended in smoke. After this England appeared to drift towards Germany and in 1899 Chamberlain attempted a *rapprochement* with Germany but met with a humiliating rebuff from Bülow.*

* Bernhard von Bülow (Prince, 1905) became German Foreign Secretary in 1897

When King Edward went to Paris only two years later public opinion was still turning towards Germany. It must, therefore, have been difficult for the officials at the Foreign Office to readjust their ideas and turn the ship of State in the opposite direction. At the time it was only thought that the King had succeeded in settling our differences with France – nothing more. Not that the King ever contemplated doing more than that when he decided to go to Paris. He never imagined that in ten years' time it would become practically a defensive alliance. His decision to go to Paris and not Berlin during his first tour abroad was arrived at without any discussion with his responsible Ministers, but whether the Government attached no importance to his movements or not, there is no record of their having suggested Berlin or of any discussion on the question.

The visit to Italy may have astonished them if they paid any attention to these visits, as Italy was at that time one of the Triple Alliance. There was, therefore, no reason why first Portugal and then Italy should have been selected as the first objects of the King's tour in Europe. Without doubt he selected these as a screen to conceal his real object. Had he gone only to Paris it would have roused the anger of the Germans, but to take Paris on his way back from Rome seemed only natural.

The meeting of the King and Emperor took place at night after the Royal yacht had been made fast to the jetty. It was pouring with rain and pitch-dark when King Edward went on shore to inspect the guard of honour, and as I got accustomed to the darkness I found the whole pier was bristling with troops while the band thundered 'God Save the King'. It was no easy matter to inspect a guard of honour under such circumstances, but King Edward, after greeting the Emperor, went round slowly and did it very well in spite of the rain. They both returned on board the Royal yacht and then the presentation of suites began. First of all the Emperor presented his retinue, and the King had a particularly charming way of showing he remembered old faces. When it came to the King presenting all the guests on board, the Emperor also greeted old friends warmly, but when I came forward the King said 'And of course you know Fritz Ponsonby', whereupon the Emperor looked at me as if he had never seen me before in his life. He didn't even shake hands but made a little formal bow and passed

and Chancellor in 1900. His relations with the Emperor William gradually deteriorated and he resigned in 1909.

70

on to the next person. I thought that he had forgotten me, although this seemed unlikely, but in any case this did not account for my being the only person with whom he didn't shake hands. However, as there was nothing to be done about it I dismissed the whole thing from my mind.

Apparently the Emperor had taken it into his head that I was the person who always dissuaded the King from visiting Germany and that I was very anti-Germany, and he therefore wished to show how much he resented my hostile attitude. His refusal to shake hands with me seemed so trivial that I wondered whether all I was told was true, but an incident occurred the next night after dinner which left no doubt whatever as to the Emperor's feelings towards me.

We dined on board the *Hohenzollern* which was really a man-of-war fitted out as a yacht. This was always a sore point with the Emperor who envied the comfort of the *Victoria & Albert*. I was talking to Captain O'Callaghan when Prince Henry of Prussia came up and we began a friendly discussion on some trivial matter. The Emperor, hearing laughter, came up and asked his brother what we were discussing. When he was told he joined in at once and gave his opinion. There was a pause when he concluded his remarks and I chipped in with some light jest which made the others laugh, but the Emperor turned towards me, looked straight at me, and then turned on his heel and walked away.

I told the King about this and he chuckled and said that the Emperor wished to be offensive to someone and had selected me. He had, of course, noticed the incident when the Emperor refused to shake hands with me.

Selborne as Minister in Attendance was in mortal fear of being offered the Red Eagle and wished me to make it clear that as a Cabinet Minister he was precluded from accepting a decoration. He said St John Brodrick had been so unmercifully chaffed at being given it, and *Punch* had had such a very funny skit on him, that he hoped there would be no mistake about it. But the first morning when he went to his cabin after breakfast there it was on his table, sent by command of the Emperor. He arrived in my cabin pale with rage and gasping maledictions. He explained that he particularly wished to avoid having to refuse it, and now he was placed in the impossible position of having either to accept it or write a letter of refusal. He certainly blamed me for putting him in this position, but I explained that I too had found the Red Eagle on my table and that although the Emperor

71

was always in a hurry with decorations, it was impossible for me to foresee that he would send them while we were in breakfast. I rang for the steward and enquired how the Red Eagles had apparently dropped from the sky through our portholes, as I had seen no emissary from the Emperor. He replied that a naval officer had come from the *Hohenzollern* while we were at breakfast and had asked to be allowed to leave decorations from the Emperor in each cabin. I told him to go at once to the officer of the watch and tell him that the Emperor's naval A.D.C. was to be prevented from leaving the yacht until I had seen him, and meanwhile all the Red Eagles were to be collected from the cabins and brought to me.

Selborne seemed pacified by my efforts but still questioned my ability to stop his particular Red Eagle. Meanwhile many of the guests seemed to resent my taking their Red Eagles from them and crowded round my cabin asking for an explanation. I, however, went off at once to catch the Emperor's A.D.C., and ran him down in the wardroom where he was being entertained by the officers of the yacht. I explained to him that according to the regulations we were not allowed to accept foreign decorations without special permission of the King, and that although I was sure this would be forthcoming I had been obliged to collect all the decorations the Emperor had so kindly sent us. If he would kindly leave me the list I would at once see the King and ask for his permission. On receiving the list I pointed out to him that Selborne, as a Cabinet Minister, was not allowed ever to accept foreign decorations, and asked him to explain this to Count Eulenburg, head of the Emperor's Household, who I knew would understand. After an hour the naval A.D.C. returned with a huge framed picture of the Emperor for Selborne and took back the First Class of the Red Eagle. Selborne was overcome with joy and one might have thought that this huge framed print of the Emperor was the one thing he had wanted all his life. So everything ended happily.

Orders and decorations played a great part in German life and the Germans were quite unable to understand English customs. The different value set on orders and decorations by us puzzled them. Whereas in Germany they gave yearly thirty thousand, in England the most that were ever given at that time was about eight hundred, and therefore a British decoration was far more difficult to get. Then on State visits foreign Sovereigns scattered three hundred to five hundred decorations, whereas the King only gave about thirty. So British decorations became like a rare stamp or rare egg, and were much sought after. Even France, a Republican country, scattered decorations during State visits, and President Loubet gave six hundred Legion of Honours when he went to St Petersburg.

The first night after dinner on board the *Hohenzollern* Count Eulenburg came up to me and became as affectionate as an old friend. He said that of course he knew all about our customs about decorations, but might he send me a list of officials who he thought might be decorated? I replied certainly, as long as he realized that the King didn't give decorations on European principles.

Soon after Richthofen, the Secretary of State, went through practically the same conversation. Finally Prince Bülow, the Chancellor, came up and said he understood the others were 'helping me' with the question of decorations, might he do the same and send me a list, although he knew how ridiculous all these trifles were?

The next day I received the lists and found there were about two hundred names on each list. I showed the lists to the King and repeated to him the purpose of the various conversations I had had. He said he wondered how men who pretended to know British customs could seriously produce long lists of persons the majority of whom were not even at Kiel but in Berlin. He added that in order to avoid unpleasantness he would give one decoration to each Minister and they were to choose the person on their list to whom it was to be given, but he stipulated that the person should be at Kiel and not in Berlin.

The next evening I had a distinctly unpleasant time. To begin with, Eulenburg came up and said, 'Is it all right about my list?' and I replied 'No, it is all wrong'. I explained that only one decoration would be given, and he bowed and retired hurt; the same thing happened with Richthofen and Bülow, who were icy in their attitude towards me. The friendly spirit had evaporated and we were back on bowing terms.

The Germans were natural decoration-hunters, as, continually wearing uniform, decorations meant so much to them, and when the alluring prospect of receiving a rare decoration was torn from them, they determined to put up a fight. All the disappointed went to their respective chiefs and said there must be some mistake: obviously the whole thing was in the hands of an ignoramus who understood nothing about the European conventionalities on State visits. Bülow, Richthofen and Eulenburg, having burnt their fingers once, had no intention of doing anything more, but they suggested that the senior officers should approach Sir Frank Lascelles. The following day poor Lascelles had a hectic time; high Court officials, Admirals, Generals, etc., tackled him and told him the whole decoration question was being mismanaged. He was a very experienced diplomatist and knew all about decorations. He merely pointed out that we did not give decorations on the German principles, but that he would make enquiries. He came to me and was much amused at what I told him about these three big men having sent me long lists. He said they had laid themselves open to a snub and they had got one. He quite approved of all I had done, but made one or two suggestions about the Kiel authorities.

The decoration-hunters, finding they could get no change out of Lascelles, went off to Metternich, their own Ambassador in London, who was the guest of the Emperor on board the *Hohenzollern*, but he was far too wily an old bird to burn his fingers with a question of this sort. I was in my cabin on board the *Victoria & Albert* when a bluejacket announced that Metternich had come on board to see me. I at once went on deck and greeted him, but when I asked him to come down to my cabin he said how much nicer it would be to sit on deck. Two armchairs were sent for and he then suggested our sitting on the upper deck of all, as it was nice being in the sun, etc. There we sat and talked of every conceivable subject: Cowes, yachting, hunting, shooting, London society, and finally foreign politics. I wondered when he was coming to the point as it seemed inconceivable that he should merely talk about trivialities, and was on my guard for fear of a trap. When we got to the European situation I was all attention, but he seemed to avoid the relations between England and Germany, which might have been interesting. I let him do the talking and merely kept the ball rolling. After half an hour he rose and said he must be going. As he went down the gangway he said, 'Is it all right about the decorations?', and when I replied 'Yes', off he went.

Afterwards I learnt that he had been so bullied by all the disappointed that he had finally consented to go and plead their case with me. The reason he had insisted on going to the upper deck was that he was conscious that telescopes and glasses from the *Hohenzollern* and other ships were fixed on him to see that he was really carrying out his promise. He wanted to give the impression that he was pleading their case and begging for decorations, while he was really talking to me about yachting, and as he was engaged with me for half an hour they were all under the impression that they had a most persistent advocate.

★   ★   ★

When we left Kassel something went wrong with the third carriage in which I was to drive to the station. Reischach came to me and asked if I would mind coming down to the station in a bus with him and some others. I replied certainly. When the King and the Emperor had driven off through the line of troops with torches, with the band thundering 'God Save the King', Reischach told me to follow him and took me round the corner to a big bus. We got in and quickly the bus filled with German officers, but it was dark and I could not see who they were. Last of all a big Prussian General climbed in and as he sat down he said, 'Gott sei Dank! Diese verfluchten Engländer sind weg' ('Thank God these cursed Englishmen are off'). Reischach at once saw he must do something to prevent the conversation continuing in this dangerous strain, and promptly presented me to all the officers in the bus. It only took a few minutes to reach the station, during which time I was unable to think of a stinging reply and translate it into German. The only replies that occurred to me were distinctly rude. I told the King about this when we got into the train and he appeared to be disappointed at my lack of repartee, but added that if the Germans came to Windsor he was sure that when they left I should say 'Thank God these d——d Germans are off'.

It was properly the duty of our King to pay the first visit to the Czar, but the Czar, being the nephew, insisted on coming on board the *Victoria & Albert* first. The King gave orders that the ladder and the steam launch were to be got ready as soon as we anchored, but of course we had no chance as the Czar's boat put off and was almost alongside before we could lower the ladder. He came on board and greeted his uncle and aunt most affectionately. After he returned to the *Polar Star* the King returned the visit and we all accompanied him. The Russian yacht was most beautifully fitted up, but there were elaborate military arrangements on board. There was a guard of honour of Russian sailors, and the King, who knew the custom, advanced to them and said in Russian, 'Good morning, my children', and the whole of the Russian sailors replied 'God save the King', also in Russian. We were then given some kirsch, which tasted like boot varnish, and caviare sandwiches. After luncheon we returned on board the Royal yacht. I saw the head of our police who asked me what steps he ought to take to ensure the safety of Their Majesties. I told him to get into a boat and go and see the head of the Russian police, whose name was Azeff and who afterwards became a famous *agent provocateur*. This he did and they recommended that an officer should be on every gangway on the yacht so as to see who came on board, as uniform was no criterion. It was absolutely necessary that every individual should be scrutinized and passed before allowing him on board the yacht. Instructions were accordingly given by Colin Keppel. In the evening we dined on board the *Polar Star*. It was rather weird, being broad daylight, as the sun apparently does not set till half-past eleven at night, and there was a beautiful red sky. The King as usual made a most impressive speech proposing the health of the Emperor, and this time I did not trust to anybody else to take down the speech, but did it myself. Afterwards we stood about on the deck while the band played. I talked to several Russians and was introduced to Stolypin,* a grave, splendid-looking man with a long grey beard. They told me that although the Nihilists had pledged themselves to kill him, he went about as if nothing had happened. It was only two years ago that his daughter was blown up, but he said that if he lived in fear of his life, life would not be worth living. He asked me a good deal about English politics and appeared to be very well up in all that was going on in England.

We were forbidden to go on shore, which was very tiresome, as I should very much have liked to see the town of Reval, which looked most picturesque. That evening the Emperor and Empress dined on board with a large suite. There were so many that a certain number had to dine in the officers' room and I was put in charge of this dinner. After dinner the two monarchs and their suites stood on deck while a steamer full of some choral society came and sang weird Russian songs. I had asked the head of our police whether this was quite safe, since the Emperor had given them permission to come within a few yards of the yacht, and Mr Quinn went off to consult the head of the Russian police, who told him that there was no danger at all. He had given orders that all the singers were to be stripped and searched before they were allowed to come on board the steamer.

When Mr Quinn came and told me this I felt there might be a row

* Minister-President of Russia, 1906–11. His confidence in his immunity from attack was misplaced; in 1911 he was shot in a theatre at Kiev, before the eyes of the Imperial family, and died shortly afterwards.

in England and questions might be asked in the House about it. The greater part of the singers were ladies, and I wondered what would be said if, when the Russian Emperor came to England and some ladies' choral society asked leave to serenade him, our police insisted on stripping them and searching them. I therefore told Mr Quinn to go back to the head of the Russian police and say that although I hoped every possible precaution would be taken, I felt this was rather too strong a measure. Mr Quinn came to me and reported later on in the evening that the Russian police had agreed to give up this stringent measure. The Emperor and Empress said goodbye to the King and we all shook hands warmly with the Russian suite, and the next morning we left for England.

★   ★   ★

In December I went to Sandringham for the Queen's birthday. On occasions of this sort the guests had to do something or say they were doing something, as the King liked to think all his guests were being amused. It was quite enough to say, 'I am going to watch the golf'; that passed, but unless some answer was given the King thought out some amusement which really bored the guest stiff.

Always when the King went out partridge-driving it was also the duty of the Equerry to ask each guest at the end of the drive how many birds they had got. On one occasion when the Equerry-in-Waiting was ill I had to perform the duty of informing guests where the King had placed them. I told Lord Rosebery that he had drawn a number between De Grey and Harry Chaplin, and he said he knew what would happen, and that was that De Grey would shoot all his birds and Harry Chaplin would pick them all up. Only birds that had actually been picked up counted. This may have been very amusing for the good shots, but it seemed to hold up the bad shots to ridicule when the totals were read out at luncheon.

Luncheon out shooting was in a large tent and everybody staying in the house had to come no matter what they might have been doing during the morning. Carriages were ordered and we all had to have luncheon in a damp tent. Tea was a full-dress meal with all the women in tea-gowns and the men in short black jackets and black ties. Gottlieb's band played like a bee in a bottle for an hour. Then everyone played games, but those who knew the routine tiptoed off to the library and read or talked. Dinner was magnificent with all the women in tiaras, etc., and all the men with ribands and decorations. Bridge had just become the fashion and the King walked round to see that everyone was engaged. The Queen went to bed soon after midnight and the King between one and one-thirty. I was told that in the old days of baccarat he used to sit up till four or five in the morning and all the men of the party had to remain up whether they were playing or not. The usual practice for those who didn't play was to go to sleep in the billiard-room with a footman specially warned to wake them when the baccarat was over.

When he came to the throne he was always very particular about members of the Household sitting up. No lady could retire before Queen Alexandra went to bed and no man could go to bed before he himself went. Usually Queen Alexandra retired about midnight, and one night early in his reign he walked through the drawing-rooms after she had gone to make sure no man had also left. He counted heads and found there was one short but could not remember who was in waiting. He rang for a page and told him that there should be so many gentlemen in the drawing-rooms but there appeared to be one short: the page was to find out who it was and go and fetch him back. It turned out to be General Sir Dighton Probyn, aged seventy-five, who had not felt well and had gone to bed. The page, however, woke him up and told him the King wanted him. King Edward, who had imagined it was one of the younger guests, was very much amused at this, but Sir Dighton was not.

★　　★　　★

In October 1906 the King went from Balmoral to stay with the Colebrookes* at Abingdon. The house was quite new, the old one having been burnt down some years previously, and everything was beautifully done, the cooking being especially good. I thought at the time that Lady Colebrooke was the genius of the establishment, but I found later that it was entirely Tommy. We went out grouse-shooting ᵐ ℬℯᵣ every day and the last day M. Poklewski-Koziell, the first Secretary of the Russian Embassy, joined the party. No one knew whether he was safe or not, and as grouse-driving is a particularly dangerous type of shooting, the King was consulted. He at once hit upon a solution and

* Edward, 1st Lord Colebrooke. Lord-in-Waiting, 1906–11; later Permanent Lord-in-Waiting to King George V.

suggested that Poklewski should be placed on the right of the line and I should go next to him to see whether he was safe. I didn't care much about this as, if he was not a safe shot, I should only find this out by being peppered. It reminded me of a Shah of Persia who on a visit to England was shown the gallows, which interested him very much. He asked whether he could see it in use, but the Governor of the gaol said that unfortunately they had no one who was to be hanged. 'That is all right. Take one of my suite!' exclaimed the Shah.

★   ★   ★

In January 1907 the King and Queen went to stay with the Duke and Duchess of Devonshire at Chatsworth where an enormous party had been invited to meet them. Everything was managed in a most princely way, and the dinners were a wonderful sight. All the women wore tiaras and jewels, while the men wore Orders and decorations. While everything was beautifully managed, anything that was left to the Duke to decide was invariably forgotten. For instance, with so large a party it was impossible for all the men to shoot, and yet the Duke never selected the guns till very late at night, and so the list was only made known the next morning. Lord Rosebery who was staying there once came down to breakfast in shooting clothes when he happened to meet his valet who said, 'You had better take those clothes off, my lord, as you are not on the shooting list.' Rosebery was furious, and immediately left for London. No one also could discover the principle on which the guns were chosen, but of course there was no principle. If the Duke happened to be sleepy he simply said the same guns as before, so that men who had been left out the first day and imagined they would have their turn, found themselves again omitted on the second day.

★   ★   ★

Later we went to stay with the Duke of Devonshire at Lismore Castle, a medieval-looking place with a courtyard and banqueting hall, but the weather was very bad and almost every day we had torrents of rain. The Duke as a host amused me, as he never took the slightest trouble with his guests and left them severely alone. He never by chance said 'Thank you' to any servant who helped him, and generally ignored anyone who might prove tiresome. At the same time he was one of the most delightful of men to talk to and could, when he chose, be the best of company.

The agent was wonderful and mapped out the programme every day, never making a mistake. King Edward therefore decided to give him the M.V.O. At that time the Victorian Order was comparatively new; and like all new Orders had come in for a certain amount of ridicule in the Press, and amusing stories invented by witty stockbrokers. When I therefore asked the Duke of Devonshire whether he approved of his agent being decorated, he replied in a sleepy way, 'Is that what they call the M.V.O.? If it is I'm sure he wouldn't like to have that.' I convinced him, however, that unless there was some political reason that would make it difficult for the agent to accept an Order from the King, I was quite sure that it would give the greatest pleasure. The Duke gave way, saying he didn't understand anything about Orders, and the agent was quite delighted with the M.V.O.

★   ★   ★

Before dinner the third night the King told me that he intended to give the Duke the Grand Cross of the Victorian Order. Knowing how little the Duke knew or cared about such things and nervous lest he should make disparaging remarks about the King's personal Order, I determined to prepare him for the honour. I went to his writing-room where I found him at his writing-table, and after discussing with him some letters he had received I told him of the King's intention to confer the Victorian Order upon him. He asked in a sleepy way what he was expected to do with 'the thing' when he got it. I replied that he must wear it and certainly that night he should wear it instead of the Garter. Anyone less anxious to receive an Order I had never seen, and I had to explain that the King looked upon his personal Order as a high honour, but the Duke seemed to think it would only complicate his dressing. Before dinner the King sent for him and handed him the Order when I believe he suitably expressed his thanks, but he straightway came to my room and asked me to put the Order on properly for him. He said that he presumed that if he wore the Victorian Order, he should not wear any part of the Order of the Garter. I was not prepared for such a difficult conundrum but I told him I had always understood that Knights of the Garter should always wear that Order on all occasions. I therefore suggested that he should wear that night not only the Riband and Star of the Victorian Order but also the Garter Star and diamond Garter on his leg. He said all this seemed complicated and tiresome but he followed my advice and the King seemed to approve as he made no comment.

★　　★　　★

I remember on one occasion the King decided to have *déjeuner* at some restaurant at St Cloud, where there was a garden and parties of people had *déjeuner* in arbours round the garden. We were a mixed party, half English and half French. Reggie Lister, the Secretary at the British Embassy, George and Alice Keppel, were among the English, and the Breteuils and Mme Standish among the French. We met the guests in the hall where we left our hats and coats and walked out in the garden to our arbour. On each side of us were parties having *déjeuner*, and Alice Keppel became nervous as she said one of them in the party on our right had a villainous face. She argued in a whisper that anyone could come in through the gate at the end of the garden, and wondered whether it was quite safe. I replied that there was ample protection from the police, but she insisted that this could not be so as they would never have allowed an obvious criminal to be so near the King. She was convinced I had given the police the wrong name of the restaurant and that there we were at the mercy of any apache who fancied robbery and any anarchist who loved assassination. At last I determined to make sure, and having hidden my handkerchief in my trouser pocket, I went through the pantomime of a man who has lost one. Finally I got up and said I wanted to get my handkerchief, which I had left in my coat. As I went back through the hall I passed the inside dining-room and there I saw Lépine himself having *déjeuner*. I went in and asked him if he was satisfied with the police arrangements, and he told me the gardener working by the garden gate was a police officer who had orders to admit no one. I said that I was not quite happy about the luncheon parties on either side, particularly the one on the right, and he laughed and said they were all police and their wives. He guessed we were nervous about one, but he said he was a *bon garçon* and one of the best and most trusted detectives in the force. I returned with my handkerchief waving and murmured to Alice Keppel that all was well, and when after luncheon I told her what Lépine had said, she could only express admiration for the methods of the French police.

81

One day the King went out by himself in the motor and the courier told me confidentially he was going to the Jardin des Plantes to meet a friend who had been a noted beauty in Paris. I telephoned to Lépine and suggested that there should on this occasion be no police in the gardens but possibly they might remain outside. He, however, objected on the grounds that an apache might see His Majesty, recognize him, and attempt to rob him. I therefore agreed to two plain-clothes men being sent there, but stipulated they should be men the King didn't know by sight.

The whole thing, however, came out very unluckily. Lépine had sent two men whom the King had never seen, but unfortunately one of them was taken ill and decided to go off at once to hospital. On his way he happened to meet one of the detectives who usually went about with the King and who offered to take his place. The King was walking with the lady when he caught sight of the detective he knew and this completely spoilt the romance of the assignation. When he got back to the hotel he asked me how I knew where he was going and why I had warned the police. I replied that it was quite by chance I knew where he was going and that naturally I had warned Lépine, who considered it was dangerous for him to be without any protection and had taken the usual precautions. He contented himself by remarking that he would take good care another time I did not know his movements, and after blowing off steam about the absurdity of the police shadowing him in Paris of all places, he never alluded to the incident again. But after that he not only tried to dodge the police but also to dodge me. He would order the motor at four and then change his mind suddenly and send for it at three, when he would slip out before anyone was ready. But these tricks were useless with the French police, and although they were caught napping the first time, they had motors ready at any time and had no difficulty in following him.

On May 1st the King, accompanied by du Bos, a great man on the turf, Johnny Ward and myself, went to see M. Blanc's racing stable. We arrived at what appeared to be a village but which was only the racing stable in attractive buildings with everything done in the most extravagant way. Afterwards we went on to luncheon at St Cloud, and du Bos's son joined us, but we said goodbye to Blanc at his stables. Later on at the races the King was surrounded by all the big swells of the French turf and I was amused to see that they never allowed Blanc to come near His Majesty, because he was a *nouveau riche* and therefore not a member of the Jockey Club.

One day the King went to visit the ex-Empress Eugénie at the Grand Hôtel, which seemed a noisy sort of place for her to stay. He took me with him and said he would wait in the motor while I enquired whether it would be convenient for her to receive him, but of course I was to use the incognito titles. I went to the clerk at the desk and said, 'La Comtesse de Pierrefonds, est elle chez elle?', and he replied, looking at the list, that she was. I asked him to ascertain whether she would receive 'Le Duc de Lancastre', but this conveyed nothing to him, and he said 'Qui ça?' I wrote it down on a piece of paper and handed it to him, but all he said was 'Bientôt'. He apparently expected me to sit down and wait while he went on sorting a packet of letters and putting them in pigeon-holes, but I was conscious all the time of the monarch fretting with impatience in a motor in the courtyard. So I told the clerk to hurry up as I was pressed for time, but he only said he must do the letters first. There was nothing for it but to drop the incognito and make him move. 'C'est le Roi d'Angleterre qui demande si l'Impératrice Eugénie veut bien le recevoir.' This had the desired effect and he went off at once. It appeared later that he was so confused and incoherent that he failed to make the Empress understand who it was. Anyhow, the answer was that the Empress would be pleased to receive him. I went outside and found the King champing his bit at being kept waiting so long. I took him into the hotel and straight to the lift. Of course, he was so accustomed to everyone making way for him that although he was incognito it never occurred to him that anyone would not do so. It happened that as we arrived at the lift a prosperous-looking American with a large cigar in his mouth decided to go up in the lift at the same moment, and conscious that he had more or less bought the whole hotel he walked straight into the lift. The result was that he and the King collided, but weight told, as His Majesty was by far the heavier, and the American cannoned off the King and lost his balance while his cigar shot out of his mouth. He obviously had no idea who the King was and appeared to resent being hustled. As we only went up to the first floor there was hardly time for a row and the American contented himself with regarding the King distastefully. I had to talk to Madame de Arcos, the Empress's lady, while the King stayed nearly an hour.

The day before we left I had a real argument with the King, who was very angry. He decided to send a present to du Bos and get Johnny Ward to write and thank him for all the excellent arrangements he had made for visiting Blanc's stables and the races afterwards. Now du Bos, a member of the French Jockey Club and one of the leading men on the French turf, would hardly expect a present, but if one was to be given it should be a good one. As a matter of fact, the King was the most generous of men and gave lovely presents without really appreciating their relative value. Often on State visits he had given gold cigarette-cases and even gold cigarette-cases with his cypher in diamonds. When the King's valet came to me with a plain silver cigarette-case with the King's cypher in enamel on it, I told him to take it back to the King and say that I hardly thought it good enough and that I suggested His Majesty should wait till he returned to London when a better cigarette-case could be sent. The valet explained that the King had given so many presents during the yachting cruise that there was really nothing left. That seemed to be all the more reason for waiting till we returned to London.

Soon afterwards the King came in and I saw at once that he was really very angry and was trying to control himself. Slowly and deliberately he put his hat, gloves and stick on the table and then said quietly, 'Did you send me a message that the cigarette-case I had chosen was not good enough?' I trembled inwardly but replied in the affirmative. Then he went on in a voice that shook the whole hotel. He asked what I knew about Paris. How could I judge what was a correct present to give to a friend like du Bos? What knowledge had I of the presents he was accustomed to give? Yet I dared to express an opinion on what I obviously had no knowledge. This flood of oratory delivered in a deafening tone swept me off my feet and reduced me to a state of speechless terror, but I recovered as he continued his abuse of me, and when he stopped I replied that I was sorry he didn't take the same view as I had, but as he usually gave such beautiful presents to his friends it was a pity that he should give such a cheap thing to du Bos, who would no doubt show it to everyone in Paris. This so far from pacifying him raised a fresh storm, and when Johnny Ward loyally supported me I thought His Majesty would have a fit, but suddenly he calmed down and dictated a letter to Johnny Ward thanking du Bos for all the excellent arrangements he had made, etc., and asking him to accept a small souvenir from His Majesty. The King rang the bell and handed the note and the cigarette-case, which had been done up in paper, to the waiter and told him to send it off at once. He then triumphantly took up his hat, stick and gloves, and left the room, slamming the door. After dinner the King came to me waving a letter with triumph, and said, 'This shows what d——d nonsense you talked.' I read the letter couched in extravagant terms expressing the deepest gratitude for the truly beautiful present, etc. etc., but when I handed it back I remarked that du Bos could not well have written anything else. It was usual with the King after he had let himself go and cursed someone to smooth matters by being especially nice to them afterwards, but in this case he resented my being so outspoken and made no attempt to forgive me. It was not till years later that I understood that he had really agreed with me but had been much annoyed at not being able to give something good. During the visit to Berlin when he was ill with a chill and quite unable to attend to anything, he said, 'I must leave the presents entirely to you to do, and I know you will do everything perfectly and not give anything shoddy like I did in Paris.'

At a *déjeuner* in Paris Monsieur and Madame Jean de Reszke were asked to meet the King. De Reszke, in addition to being a great singer, was a charming man with a quaint sense of humour. He had taught his wife to sing and it was said that, like Svengali in Du Maurier's novel, he in a sort of a way hypnotized her when she sang. However that may be, there is no doubt that when he accompanied her she sang divinely.

After *déjeuner* she was asked to sing, but the question arose what *should* she sing? Jean de Reszke asked the King for his favourite song, but His Majesty said he hoped she would sing anything she liked. Songs were suggested but turned down by Jean, and although I ventured to suggest modern songs by Reynaldo Hahn, Debussy and others, he always shook his head.

There seemed an impasse, but suddenly he said 'J'y suis', and suggested *La Traviata*, and this was at once approved of. He explained to me afterwards that he was determined she should sing something the King knew, and that he was quite sure His Majesty, like all that generation, knew this opera well.

One day we went round the Salon with Detaille,* who pointed out all the pictures worth seeing. I received instructions to wear a short black London coat and a tall hat. Knowing how particular the King was about dress I hesitated to adopt this sort of Stock Exchange attire, but on my asking the King to make sure I had not got his message

* Edouard Detaille, the celebrated painter of battle-pictures.

wrong, he explained it would be impossible to go in country clothes with a squash hat, and yet a frock-coat would be out of place. He therefore always went to see pictures in a short coat and top-hat. My brain gave way under the strain of grasping these niceties of dress.

Detaille, like de Reszke, in addition to being a great artist, was a delightful human being and very good company. His comments on the pictures were always amusing and he never spared the artist in his criticisms. When we entered one of the rooms we came across a very bad picture and the King began asking why they admitted such daubs, when Detaille coughed loudly and said it was a very fine picture. The King at once tumbled to it that something had happened and remained silent. Detaille thereupon called up a man who was standing near and presented him to the King. He was the artist of the daub.

We went to luncheon with the Breteuils in their beautiful house in the Avenue du Bois de Boulogne, and I sat between Madame Pourtales and Lépine, the head of the police. I always think the French system of meals may be very good for people who have nothing to do and are only out for amusement, but for busy people they are most inconvenient. I had *café au lait* at 8 a.m. with one roll and butter. Therefore by 12.45, when we had *déjeuner*, I was so hungry that I ate every dish and was quite incapable of doing any work in the afternoon. I wanted either to talk or go to sleep. Of course, the ordinary Frenchman does have a siesta, but that means he does no work till four or five.

The King's position in Paris was really most remarkable. He was credited with enormous powers and the fact that he was a constitutional Sovereign was entirely lost sight of. He was regarded as an autocrat, and in Paris where the people had a craving for hero-worship but had no hero, they placed him on a pedestal and worshipped him. He knew so well how to manage the two entirely distinct worlds in Paris – the Social and the Official world, and never made the mistake of getting them mixed. If it was a State visit or any municipal function, he ignored the Faubourg St Germain, but on the other hand, when going out to luncheon or dinner, he never expressed any desire to meet the official world.

The King of the Belgians was in Paris at the time and, knowing the King disliked him, he never showed any signs of life. It was therefore very bad luck that he should hit on the same play on the same night as the King. We dined at Voisin's, the King, the Ambassador, Lady Feo Bertie, Reggie Lister, Alice Keppel, Johnny Ward and myself, and afterwards went to see Granier in *Bonne Intention*. When we entered our box I caught sight of King Leopold, who sank as low as he could in the stalls, like a hare in a field when shooting is going on. However, there was no reason why the two Kings should meet.

The Press was a constant difficulty; every evening I issued a rough statement of what the King had done during the day while I begged reporters to refrain from publishing details of private visits. On that particular night I merely said 'le Roi dîne en ville', and the more respectable papers repeated this, but the yellow Press came to the conclusion that as both Kings were at the same theatre they must have dined together. They therefore published fictitious accounts of the two monarchs having dinner together; this annoyed King Edward quite enormously, although I explained how difficult it was to prevent this sort of thing happening and how inadvisable it would be to publish a denial.

This was the last night we spent in Paris and I had to sit up till three in the morning to clean up all the work, as it was impossible to leave anything to stand over.

★　　★　　★

The Abbot of Tepl, a great dignitary of the Roman Catholic Church, asked the King to shoot and the idea seemed to tickle His Majesty. But the Abbot's idea of shooting was rather primitive; he imagined that you had only to buy a certain number of partridges, put them down in a field, drive them over the guns, and all would go well. The ranger who was to manage the shoot, however, told him that the danger was that the partridges might fly away early in the morning. He therefore recommended that two kites should be flown over the field; the partridges would mistake them for big birds and refuse to fly. Unfortunately they left the kites still flying when the beaters began the drive, with the result that the partridges absolutely refused to get up and fly and either ran or else flew low and constantly alighted. This made the shooting very difficult as the birds remained close in front of the beaters. As a shoot it was a fiasco; but as a day out in the country it was amusing. The King for some obscure reason was placed on the right and hardly got a shot, and I asked the other guns how many birds they had shot and made out we had a total bag of 36 brace, but later I found that the ranger had counted all the birds that had died in the train or been knocked on the head by the beaters, so that eventually a game-card was framed showing that the bag had been 150 brace. The guns were the King, Prince Lucinge, Eddy Stonor,★ Arthur Boyd, Ernest Scott, Seymour Fortescue and myself. One old monk came out with an old-fashioned gun and a bag of cartridges. This alarmed Eddy Stonor, who asked him where he intended to go. He replied he was going by himself behind the beaters and added, 'It will all be quite safe, but of course if anyone shoots at me, I shall shoot back.'

★ ★ ★

The next year, 1907, we arrived at Marienbad on August 19th. One night the King went to the theatre. The play on the advertisement was called *Die Hölle*.† His Majesty thought it was a melodrama, and having nothing else to do thought it would amuse him to go and see it. When we arrived, however, we found it to be a sort of music-hall performance. The actors came from a music-hall away in Vienna called 'Die Hölle'. There were nothing but songs and recitations, and I believe the songs were very improper, but the double meanings were entirely wasted on me. I was intensely bored by the performance. When the second act began very much the same as the first, with a song, the King got up and left.

The next day the papers were full of this incident. They said that the King had gone to an improper performance and had left in disgust to show his disapproval. A day or two afterwards letters came from England thanking the King for making a firm stand in the cause of morality. The people who had not been at the theatre said that the performance must have been pretty hot to make the King and myself leave. It was in vain that I said that all the improper part had been wasted on me; even people in England wrote to me and chaffed me about taking up such a very moral attitude. The Bishop of Ripon (Boyd Carpenter) wrote a letter to the King expressing the satisfaction of the whole Church at the protest the King had publicly made against obscene musical comedy. It was a very flowery letter and one would have thought that the King had made a speech on the subject, so much was made of the incident. I asked the King what reply I should send, and he said, 'Tell the Bishop the exact truth. I have no wish to pose as a protector of morals, especially abroad.'

★ Brother of Harry Stonor.
† *The Underworld*.

The King's dog, Caesar, had been ill, and His Majesty wanted to send for Sewell from London. Sewell's charge was £200 for coming out. I expostulated with the King on the extravagance of having out a man who charged so much, but His Majesty said that if his dog was ill he would get the very best man, and he did not care what it cost. Luckily a first-class vet was found in Vienna who came and cured the dog.

One evening the King dined with Mrs Hall Walker, and after dinner a new dancer came, by name Maud Allan, who had never danced in London. The King expressed a wish to see her dance, but I was rather doubtful from what I had heard as to whether it would be right for His Majesty to do so. I had been told that she danced more or less naked, and I was afraid that the English Press might get hold of this and make up some wild story. I therefore went to Mrs Walker and said that I had heard that Miss Maud Allan danced with only two oyster-shells and a five-franc piece, and questioned whether it was quite wise for the King to see her. Mrs Walker replied that Miss Allan was a great artist and that there was nothing at all offensive in the performance. The question was to get the music, and finally Little, the correspondent of the *Daily Mail*, and the leader of the town band were made to play duets for Miss Maud Allan to dance to. I went at once to Little and explained to him that he was coming in as a friend, and that I trusted that he would not report any of this in the *Daily Mail*. He roared with laughter and said that of course he would treat it quite confidentially. The dance was very exceptional, and I must say that Miss Maud Allan was really wonderful. Her dance as Salome with the head of John the Baptist was really most dramatic, and, although I cannot say she wore many clothes, there was nothing the least indecent about her performance.

★   ★   ★

The King was very kind about my golf and usually left me the afternoons free for it, but on one occasion at the last moment when someone failed he asked me to make a fourth at croquet. Croquet is a game the niceties of which I have never mastered, and although I had at various times played, I was a very bad player. To spend hours playing this game did not attract me and I determined to make myself as unpleasant as possible so that I should never be asked again. I drove up with the King to the croquet-ground, which was part of the Golf

89

Club, and found that the game had already been arranged, His Majesty and Madame Letellier against old Harry Chaplin and myself. We played for two and a half hours and whenever I got the chance I sent the King's ball to the other end of the ground. This made him quite furious, and the beautiful Madame Letellier, who was quite a good player, begged me with tears in her eyes not to make him so angry, adding that she understood that courtiers always allowed monarchs to win. I replied that this was out of date and that personally I always made a point of beating the Royal Family at any game if I possibly could. I continued my tactics although it made the game distinctly unpleasant. Harry Chaplin, who had played in his youth, seemed to know all about the game and so we went ahead and looked like winners, but Madame Letellier was too good for us. Just as we were winning she caught us up and made things so awkward that we were held up. Then the King did several hoops and caught us up. We had a very exciting finish and they just won on the post. To my horror the King said that this was by far the best game he had had and that therefore we would have a return match the next day. However, he afterwards relented and said that as he knew I disliked croquet he would get someone else.

During this visit to Marienbad, Clemenceau, then Premier of France, was taking the cure at Karlsbad. He seemed to get on extremely well with the King. It was very tiresome, but I suppose inevitable, that he should be making constant statements to the Press, who gathered round him like flies. Wickham Steed,★ *The Times* man, told me he had had a special interview and Clemenceau had talked very openly. This, of course, was on a higher plane than the statements to journalists. Marienbad prided itself on being the place where important conversations were held, but hitherto nothing had ever been published.

One day Clemenceau came to luncheon and was brilliantly witty and amusing, talking on every conceivable subject. His views on golf were distinctly original. He said that he knew all about English games and sports. They were only an excuse for bringing the young man and the young woman together and there was nothing in them but that. Did he not often see a *partie de croquet* with young people really engaged in making love? Tennis was very much the same: the young man tried to show how athletic he was, but the real objective was to

★ Later Editor of *The Times* and author of *The Hapsburg Monarchy*.

sit out afterwards with a young lady. When, however, it came to golf he admitted that his theory didn't apply. He once was at La Boulie golf ground near Paris and he saw a young man and woman starting off for golf. He thought that this was only an excuse for a delightful walk in the woods with infinite possibilities in the way of love-making, but he saw the young man go off to the left and the young girl to the right and they never seemed to get together at all.

At the end of luncheon he became serious and outlined the next big war when Germany would certainly walk straight on Paris and demand a huge indemnity. He said he had asked Edward Grey★ what the British Empire would do if Germany went through Belgium to Paris, and Grey replied undoubtedly it would create a great stir in England. That, Clemenceau said, would be a lot of use to France. He was warming up to his subject when the King, fearing indiscretions, asked him to come to his room and have a talk.

Prince Danilo of Montenegro† was also in Marienbad about this time, and was what the Scotch call 'a puir wratch'. The King asked him to luncheon but beyond that did not take much notice of him in spite of Prince Danilo's efforts. The Prince asked me to tell the King that the dearest wish of his heart was to have a British Order, and that although he had been several days at Marienbad this had not materialized. I replied that the King was incognito and that any idea of giving decorations was out of the question, but he argued that everyone in his own country would consider it a slight if he were not to return with a British Order.

I repeated all this to the King, who said he had never heard such impudence. Did Prince Danilo really imagine that British decorations were chucked about like this? If he did, the sooner he learnt our customs the better.

Prince Danilo had arranged with me that if the answer was favourable I was to come up to him and shake hands when he came to say goodbye to the King, but if unfavourable I was to take no notice of him. When he finally came to take leave of His Majesty I remained immovable and looked at the ceiling. I was conscious, however, of his glaring at me the whole time.

★　　★　　★

★ Later 1st Viscount Grey of Fallodon. Foreign Secretary, 1905–15.
† Crown Prince of Montenegro.

The programme for the three days' State visit was a heavy one. In addition to the family luncheons and dinners, there was a civic reception at the Brandenburg Gate, luncheons with the 1st Prussian Dragoon Guards and the British Ambassador, a Court ball, a motor drive to Potsdam, a gala performance at the Opera, and a visit to the Rathaus.

The visit to the Rathaus was very interesting. The whole building was crammed with people, and the Burgomaster made a long speech and presented an album in a case. The King replied in German, and there was breathless silence. At the conclusion of his speech he received enthusiastic applause.

That evening there was a gala dinner which was magnificently done, and the King and the Emperor spoke. I think that the King, fearing what the Emperor might say, insisted on both speeches being seen by the other beforehand, and read instead of spoken. We then retired into a long gallery where I spoke to all sorts of people I knew. The ball then began, and we returned to the Weisser Saal and witnessed all sorts of extraordinary old-fashioned dances. There was something ludicrous about German officers in modern uniform dancing minuets, but as the Emperor explained to me afterwards, people did not come to a Court ball to amuse themselves but to learn deportment. After the ball we went to supper, which was served at a large number of small tables in various rooms. All of us were placed among the Princes and Princesses. At my table were two of the Emperor's sons, and various Princesses, who explained to me that they had tried to introduce the two-step, and while the Emperor was at supper they had instructed the band to play some well-known tune. The Emperor heard it and there was a proper row.

To my mind the effect of this visit was nil. One felt that a few charming men really liked us, but with the majority I derived the impression that they hated us. The Germans never forgave the King for having, as they imagined, isolated them from the rest of Europe. They attributed to him the fact that Germany practically stood alone in the councils of Europe. The Emperor for his part seemed to do all he could to make the visit a success, but he was never at his ease with the King. There were always forced jokes, and the whole atmosphere when the two were together seemed charged with dangerous electricity. I really saw very little of the suite, being so busy, but what struck me particularly was the King's wonderful power of directing everything. Ill as he was, the whole suite always awaited his orders.

After being with the German Emperor some time one began to see that his brilliance was mostly superficial and all his conversation studied beforehand. It seemed to me that he anticipated what subjects of conversation would crop up and then got his staff to look out statistics, which he afterwards brought out in conversation, with the result that people were astounded at his knowledge. He was particularly good at committing statistics to memory. When he was in London he asked some Admiral what the tonnage of the new Dreadnoughts was, and when the answer was not absolutely correct he corrected it, and incidentally brought in the statistics of all the latest ships in the British Navy. Everyone said how wonderful, and what profound knowledge his conversation implied, but, of course, he had just learnt these statistics up before dinner.

I must say that he caught me out properly when one day at Friedrichshof he asked me across the table how many there were on the London County Council, who were qualified to vote, and how many years elapsed between the elections. I had very vague ideas on all these questions, but I bravely answered all of them, making shots at the numbers. 'I don't think you're right,' replied the Emperor, and then he proceeded to give chapter and verse. I must say it was very effective and everyone present marvelled at his knowledge.

Quite apart from this superficial acting, the Emperor had great fascination as a conversationalist, as he was always so keen and interested. He practically stood on one's feet, glaring into one's eyes and giving grunts of approval, which acted as a spur. As a Sovereign he had learnt his work thoroughly, and I imagine that if he had to talk to an officer in charge of submarines he worked up the subject; and equally with a judge, an architect or a financier, he would prepare his subject beforehand. His sense of humour was of the blatant type and he was unable to appreciate any subtle witticism, but I have heard him tell stories which were quite funny. He was the creation of the Germans themselves. They wanted a sabre-rattling autocrat with theatrical ways, attempting to dominate Europe, sending telegrams and making bombastic speeches, and he did his best to supply them with the superman they required. He liked to be thought a superman and painted pictures, wrote sermons, arranged ballets and criticized architecture with equal dexterity, and in fact prided himself on directing every form of activity in Germany.

★   ★   ★

On February 18th, after a long day's work at Buckingham Palace, I came by chance into the Equerries' room about 11.30 p.m. and found Prince Henry of Prussia, his Equerry, Commander Von Usedom, and Cunninghame-Graham, who was attached to His Royal Highness. They were talking about charities when I came in and their talk continued for some time, when Prince Henry suddenly turned on me and said: 'Fritz, why is it we cannot get on?' I was first rather taken aback, and began generalities about the Press being responsible for the bad feeling and about commercial rivalry. Prince Henry shook his head and said: 'No, Fritz, that won't do.' So of course I was put on my mettle. I told him that it was not surprising that a feeling of distrust and suspicion had arisen when Germany insisted on building a fleet. Germany did not want a fleet to fight France or Russia or any other Power. We were therefore justified in assuming that this fleet was intended to fight England.

Prince Henry got very keen and excited and said that nothing was further from their thoughts than a war with England. They had now forty years' peace and had been able to form themselves into a nation. For the one hundred years before that they had been constantly fighting and had never had a chance. Most of the battles in the Napoleonic Wars had taken place in Germany itself. Now they were prospering, what possible object could they have in going to war with us? They had nothing to gain, and in any case it would cripple them and they would probably lose their trade. He wished people here would understand that Germany only wished to defend her commerce and that any idea of invasion was out of the question. He said that they had no plan of invasion; if such a thing was possible he wished we would explain how it could be done, but to any thinking man it must be evident that it would be impossible to send off transports full of men as long as there was even one submarine afloat.

I pointed out that, although this might be the case, he must see that a strong German Fleet threatened our national existence. We practically had no Army, and were we to lose command of the sea we should lose not only all our colonies but our independence. I said that as long as Germany continued to build we were bound to do the same, and I asked him where it was going to end. Naturally the increased taxation was being felt by all classes in both countries, and the middle class, who felt it most, were told it was on account of the German naval programme. He replied that this feeling of suspicion and distrust did not exist in Germany, and that two years ago, in order to show his

94

confidence, he had taken the whole Fleet away to Madeira and Gibraltar and had remained away two months. Yet in spite of this we insisted on massing the whole Fleet at Dover. Why did we do this? He had asked McKenna, the First Lord of the Admiralty, who had replied that it was done for motives of economy! He repeated the question to me: Why did we mass the Fleet at Dover?

I replied that a Fleet was not kept for pleasure-boats or for digging potatoes. It was kept for one purpose, i.e. war, and therefore it was only common sense that we should keep the Fleet at a point where we should be most likely to want it.

He laughed and said, 'You are the first that has dared to tell me that.' I pointed out that the fact that Germany had made all arrangements for fighting on the Russian frontier in no way implied that she had any intention of going to war with Russia. It was only common sense after all to make the best possible disposition in peace-time of forces that were intended for war.

Prince Henry agreed with this, but said that in Germany this was construed into a direct preparation for war. A large number of people in Germany had a fixed idea that England would on the slightest excuse come and smash the German Fleet, and at present they were at our mercy. All they wanted was to be able to say 'Hands off'. In any difference of opinion on European questions they had to take what we dictated 'lying down'. They had studied European history and they knew that whenever any European Power rose to any predominance, we smashed them. He instanced, the Dutch, Spaniards, and later the French. They did not in Germany mean to follow the example of the others.

They had no wish for war, but they did not mean to remain defenceless and at our mercy. It was absurd to think that they wished in any way to compete with us. All they did want was to be strong enough to hold their own in the event of our attacking them.

I saw Mr Asquith the next day and he told me that Prince Henry had asked to see him and discuss relations between the two countries. I told him of my conversation and he begged me to let him have a précis of it. He added that he hoped Prince Henry would not be so outspoken, as he might have to tell him some home truths.

I therefore sent him a typed copy describing the conversation, and two days after I saw him at the State Ball. He came up and thanked me. He said it had been of the greatest use to him, although Prince Henry had been much more guarded in his conversation. He had sent it to the Foreign Office and the Admiralty, and had asked for facts and figures so that he might make no mistake.

Years later, when the War broke out, I reminded Asquith of this conversation and asked him whether he thought Prince Henry a fool or a knave: that is to say, had he been made a fool of by Admiral Tirpitz, who had told him that he must go to England to allay all suspicion, or did he know the true facts and was he merely posing as a candid friend to conceal Germany's warlike intentions? Asquith replied he thought the latter. Prince Henry was no fool, and Tirpitz must have told him all his plans. It was clear, therefore, that he had agreed to go to England and through me to get the German view conveyed to the King. Personally I came to the conclusion that Prince Henry's visit had in no way been instigated by Tirpitz, and that, being a genuine friend of England, he had tried his best to smooth matters. He was a perfectly straightforward man and never gave one the impression of having any Machiavellian cunning.

★   ★   ★

Out of the blue in 1910, a message arrived that the King wished to speak to me. I was very nervous, but rushed upstairs. I was told he was in the audience-room where he saw Ambassadors, etc., a room with red brocade on the walls and many well-known pictures by old masters. As I was accustomed to see him in his work-room, which was next door, this made me more nervous than ever, and when I entered I found no one there. I grasped that I had arrived too soon, and when I heard the King's voice in his bedroom saying, 'That will do, I must go now', I thought it best to retire and wait outside. After two or three minutes more the nurse came out to see if I was there, and I entered the room trying to look as if everything was as usual. I found the King sitting at his writing-table with a rug round his legs, and I was rather shocked with his appearance. His colour was grey and he appeared to be unable to sit upright and to be sunken. At first he had difficulty with his breathing and was like a man out of breath, but this gradually got better. He said he would sign what there was in the boxes, and I proceeded to open them and handed him documents for his signature. They were merely routine submissions, and he signed these one after the other and seemed to like the work. Even the Foreign Office telegrams he read, but I kept back some documents that would have necessitated a discussion and therefore conversation. I then tried to leave the room, but he wanted to know what had happened at my meeting about the inspection of the Boy Scouts. I again tried to go, but he said in a gasping voice, 'You managed so well at Biarritz. I hope everyone was thanked.' Then, after a painful pause, 'Especially the Press.' I told him I had thanked them all. I said in as cheerful voice as I could command that I hoped he would soon be better. He replied, 'I feel wretchedly ill. I can't sleep, I can't eat. They really must do something for me.'

I was to be relieved the next day by Arthur Davidson, and the extraordinary thing was that, ill as he was, he remembered this. He turned to me and said, 'In case I don't see you again, goodbye.' I shook him by the hand, but I do not think that he meant anything more than what he usually said when I went out of waiting.

I never saw him again, for he died the next day. Meanwhile, I went down to Tangley, my house in the country, where I had hoped to spend a few weeks with my family. Late that night I received a telephone message telling me that Queen Alexandra wished me to come up to London. I motored up at once and went upstairs at Buckingham Palace, where I met the nurse, who told me the Queen was in the King's room and that I had better wait downstairs. I had hardly descended the stairs when a page came and explained to me that the Queen was waiting for me. I went into the King's room and there I found the Queen. I attempted to kiss her hand, not from ceremony but in sympathy, but she would not allow me to do so. She thanked me for the letter I had written her, and then led me into the next room. The blinds were down and there was a screen round the bed, so that at first I could see nothing, but when we came round it I saw the poor King lying apparently asleep. His face looked natural and peaceful and there was no sign of suffering. I was very much awed and hardly liked to speak except in a whisper, but the Queen spoke quite naturally and said how peaceful he looked and that it was a comfort to think he had suffered no pain. She added that it was not Sandringham but that 'horrid Biarritz' that had killed him, although no doubt the political crisis had had something to do with it. I couldn't argue, but I knew this was not true. She said she felt as if she had been turned into stone, unable to cry, unable to grasp the meaning of it all, and incapable of doing anything. She added she would like to go and hide in the country, but there was this terrible State Funeral and all the dreadful arrangements that had to be made.

I was with her about ten minutes and when I came out I met the

97

new King and Queen. I debated in my mind what I should do, and although kissing their hands seemed a tiresome formality so out of keeping with the simplicity of Queen Alexandra's grief, and although I knew that both King George and Queen Mary disliked anything at all theatrical in private, I came to the conclusion that as everyone else had probably gone through this formality I had better go through it, too. I sank down on one knee and kissed their hands in turn.

In accordance with precedent the King's Company kept watch over the body of King Edward, and it was a most impressive sight to see them relieving guard, but there was a certain amount of jealousy in the Army at their claiming the exclusive right of this privilege. The first part of the funeral consisted in taking the body to Westminster Hall where the lying-in-state would take place. This was an innovation which proved very popular, and thousands of people formed long queues stretching far down the riverside in order to witness the sight. In addition to the King's Company, the Gentlemen-at-Arms, the Sovereign's Bodyguard, also took turns at keeping watch. The final funeral procession through London was well managed and the crowd was the largest I have ever seen. King Edward's Equerries were the pall-bearers, but as the extra Equerries were afterwards added and all sorts of officials thought they had the right to walk at the side of the gun-carriage, there was a crowd-jostling effect which was undignified. The final ceremony at Windsor was entrusted to me, and with memories of Queen Victoria's funeral only nine years earlier I found no difficulty in organization.

The gathering of Kings at Windsor was truly remarkable, and there is no record of so large a number having ever met before. In addition to the German Emperor there were the Kings of Spain,★ Portugal, Denmark, Belgium,† Norway and Bulgaria.

★   ★   ★

With King Edward's passing we lost a lovable, wayward and human monarch. He was one who came to decisions by instinct and not by logic, and rarely made a mistake in his judgement of men. On the whole, he preferred the society of the female sex and was never happier than in the company of pretty women. He always thought a

---

★ Alfonso XIII.
† King Albert, who had succeeded Leopold II in the previous year.

men's dinner party was tiresome and dull. I remember one Ascot week, after the death of the King of Denmark, it was decided to have a men's party as Queen Alexandra was in mourning, and I happened to be with him when the list of guests was sent in to him on his arrival at Windsor. He looked at it and said with a sigh, 'What tiresome evenings we shall have!'

It was on this occasion that he and Lord Rosebery had some difference of opinion the first night. I never discovered what it was all about, but the result was that while apparently it made no impression on the King, Lord Rosebery sulked and became impossible during practically the whole week. If anyone tried to draw him into conversation he turned an eye like a fish on them and withered them with biting sarcasm. So everyone avoided him. After dinner he would get a book and read, but he never joined in any of the jokes such parties produce.

The last night I happened to be at a loose end for something to do after dinner, when to my surprise he called out to me to come and talk. He suggested that as it was a fine warm night we should sit out on the terrace. I rang the bell and asked for two easy-chairs to be put out on the East Terrace, and there we went. All the pent-up mirth that had been firmly suppressed during the week came bubbling out and I cried with laughter at his witticisms. Unfortunately I laughed so loud that it attracted the attention of several of the guests, who came out on to the terrace to see what it was that had amused me so much. Soon there were a dozen or more standing round our basket arm-chairs, and Rosebery, liking an audience, became wittier and wittier. Soon the castle walls were echoing with roars of laughter. King Edward, who was playing bridge, heard these sounds of merriment and when he was dummy walked about to see the cause. To his surprise he found the other drawing-rooms practically empty and, guided by the sounds, he came out on the terrace and joined the crowd in the dark.

I suddenly recognized his laughter and jumped up and offered him my chair, but he refused it. Rosebery also got up, but remained silent. There was an awkward pause, and King Edward remarked that he must go back to his bridge. Rosebery then quietly followed and went back to his book.

The King's great attraction was that he was a very good listener. During the interviews and audiences, no matter on what subject, he was always able to fix his attention on his visitor. Men who came from Central Africa or from some other remote place were delighted at being asked questions, and came away with a great admiration for the King, who really had only listened intently; I have seen the King apparently deeply interested in something which I knew bored him.

In society it was often the King's custom to pretend to know nothing about a subject, and even to refuse to understand some obvious point connected with that subject, when all the time he knew much more than the people who were trying to explain it. I never quite understood why he assumed this attitude, but it probably was the outcome of his wish to become discreet. As Prince of Wales he was always reputed to be most indiscreet, and several instances could be quoted of his giving away secrets. The truth was that he was only occasionally told secrets, and while it is easy to be discreet when one knows everything, it is much more difficult to keep occasional bits of news secret, more especially when going about in society as King Edward did. When he became King and knew all the inner workings of all State affairs there was no one more discreet. It occurred to me, therefore, that this peculiar trait he had of professing ignorance on some comparatively trivial subject may have come from his deter-mination to become discreet.

The King had an unholy passion for decorations; not only did he revolutionize the wearing of medals and decorations in England, but his great wish was to see men wearing as many as possible. In Queen Victoria's reign foreign decorations were unknown, for she had all the old-fashioned prejudice against her subjects wearing foreign decora-tions; during the seven years I was with her I never received one, yet during King Edward's reign I received eighteen. Although possibly Queen Victoria's attitude was the right one, if any monarch travelled as King Edward did it was impossible to ignore the customs of other nations and not to give a certain number of decorations when monarchs meet; for if nothing is given there are apt to be difficulties and misunderstandings. Foreign decorations were originally given to save the expense of giving snuff-boxes, etc. A man who received a Grand Cross of some Order, value £25, was happier than a man who received a snuff-box worth £200, so monarchs saved their purses and pandered to the unwholesome craving of human beings to wear decorations which they had in no way earned.

The pleasure of giving never seemed to diminish with King Edward. Most very rich men are so imposed upon and meet with so little gratitude that they derive no pleasure after a time from being generous, and develop into stingy men, but King Edward up to the end took great pleasure in giving presents or in doing someone a kind action. He was by nature the most generous of men, and it was this trait in his character that induced him to give so many decorations. He liked the obvious pleasure it gave the recipient. At any game of cards he disliked losing intensely, but loved paying his losses and did so as if he were making his opponent a present.

He had a most curious brain and at one time one would find him a big, strong, far-seeing man, grasping the situation at a glance and taking a broadminded view of it; at another one would be almost surprised at the smallness of his mind. He would be almost childish in his views, and would obstinately refuse to understand the question at issue. It was with matters that did not interest him that he was at his worst, and he would never make the slightest effort to go into the details of anything that bored him; but with questions that interested him no detail would be too small for his attention.

I found that Foreign Affairs, the Army and the Navy interested him most, while internal politics and the Colonies bored him. He would rush through any question relating to the latter, but would read thoroughly through even insignificant letters relating to the former. He read through every dispatch from abroad, often when the subject was very dull. Any inaccuracy annoyed him: even a slip of the pen put him out.

I remember once being with him on board the yacht, and after he had carefully perused some (to my mind) very uninteresting dispatches from abroad, I handed him the basis for discussion at the Imperial Conference with a long and interesting covering letter from Alfred Lyttelton.★ He ticked it off and handed it back to me saying, 'I will take that as read.' I protested, however, that as the Colonial Premiers would be in London when he returned, and as he would meet them at dinner, it was absolutely necessary that he should master the details of their discussions. He hastily said that he had not time then, but would do so later. Feeling sure he would never take the trouble to read through all this printed matter, I made a précis of it and had it typed. This I sent to him by a page, and when I next saw him he said that it was 'no doubt very interesting' but he did not appear to have read much of it. I therefore went over the ground again, and to my amusement he turned round in his chair with a determined face: 'Yes, you are quite right. I must get hold of this.' He then gave his

★ Colonial Secretary, 1903–05.

whole mind to it and in a short time had mastered it. I think that he was grateful to me when he went to London: he talked to several of the Premiers and drew them out.

In foreign affairs he was, however, always interested. He read carefully all the blue-prints and never failed to put his finger on any weak spot there may have been. With the Army and Navy he was equally good except in the matter of uniform, where he appeared petty and small-minded; but so great was his influence in matters of dress that he revolutionized the appearance of the officers of both Services. Formerly a certain slovenliness had been the fashion, but after the King ascended the throne this was all changed and smartness and uniformity of dress became the order of the day.

I never quite understood why he made people so frightened of him, but there can be no doubt that even his most intimate friends were all terrified of him. Abroad this was more noticeable, and on the many journeys I took with him I had only to mention his name and at once all resistance vanished. Whenever he expressed any wish there was never any opposition, for he was by far the biggest man and the most striking personality in Europe.

I have seen Cabinet Ministers, Ambassadors, Generals and Admirals absolutely curl up in his presence when trying to maintain their point. As regards myself, I varied. If I was quite certain of my facts I never minded standing up to him. In fact, I always noticed that he invariably respected people who stood up to him, and he carried this so far that he was always taken in by dictatorial and cocksure people. At times, however, I was perfectly terrified of him, more especially if I was in unusual surroundings. In his business-room, standing by his chair, I was quite at home, so to speak, and found no difficulty in arguing with him, but when at luncheon or staying at a country house he got cross over a matter I knew little about, he fairly scared me.

Yet in spite of all this King Edward had that indefinable quality of making all his staff devoted to him. All his personal Household loved him and his friends were deeply attached to him. The reason was that he was intensely human and that he was a great enough man to show his friends his true self with all the weaknesses of a human being. He never posed and never pretended to be any better than he was. The upper and lower classes loved him, although the middle class were often shocked at his actions.

★ ★ ★

When George V decided to let his mother, Queen Alexandra, continue to live at the big house at Sandringham, while he and the Queen lived at York Cottage, everyone was surprised; but all the King's Household determined to make his arrangement work. Not only did the King allow his mother to live in Sandringham House, but even paid a few thousands every year to enable her to do so.

Charles Cust* got into severe trouble through speaking his mind too freely; but really what he said was quite common sense. It was reported to Princess Victoria that he had said that he thought it quite absurd that a large house like Sandringham should be inhabited by an old lady and her daughter, while tiny York Cottage should have to accommodate a married man with a family of six, more especially when the man happened to be the King. Princess Victoria said she would never forgive him for saying such unkind things and would never speak to him again. The King intervened and smoothed the ruffled waters; he told Charles Cust that he could not see what the devil it had got to do with him and, of course, there was a great deal in this.

King George V hated all insincerity and flattery, but after a time he got so accustomed to people agreeing with him that he resented the candid friend business. At one time he took a dislike to me as he thought I invariably disagreed with any views he happened to express, but after a time he regarded me as an unavoidable critic.

Anyhow, as I was doing the work of Private Secretary, I found it all very uncomfortable. I wanted very little – merely a small room with a writing-table and a telephone, and enough room for official boxes and files. This would not appear difficult; but as, in addition to the King, Queen and six children, there were a lady-in-waiting, an equerry, a governess, a tutor and myself, every available room was occupied. The servants were mostly billeted in neighbouring cottages, so that taking a servant's room was no solution.

When I first went to York Cottage the Queen asked me to use the school-room for my writing-room and also for seeing people; but after a few days I found that it was the one place where all the young princes and Princess Mary† were accustomed to meet and talk. I thought then of the billiard-room which was very little used, and

* Captain Sir Charles Cust, R.N., 3rd Bart. Equerry to King George V since 1892. Died 1931.
† The Princess Royal.

gathered up my boxes and retired there. I had hardly been there for a quarter of an hour when Prince Harry looked in and asked if he and Prince George★ could play billiards. I said of course they could and, again gathering up my papers, I retired to my bedroom and sent a footman for the boxes. I had quite a nice bedroom, although it had a very small writing-table, but there I felt safe from interruption. The Chief Constable of Norfolk came to see me and was rather surprised at being ushered into my bedroom; while he was with me, Rowland Grant, the Rector, and Beck, the agent, also came and had to sit in the passage and wait. Everything went well; but when the Chief Constable asked if he could telephone to King's Lynn, I told him he could not, as there was only a telephone in the schoolroom where the young princes were and one in the passage where everyone in the house listened to what was said.

The Queen heard of this and told me she hoped I would go back to the schoolroom, but I pointed out that it was wrong for one person to evict six selfishly and that really I was quite happy writing in my bedroom.

★   ★   ★

The King decided to present that night six medallions from Windsor. They had formerly formed part of the statue of Louis XVI and had been bought by George IV. They were in bronze and modelled by Desjardins. His Majesty told me to arrange to have them ready at the Elysée. So I got hold of Colonel Aldebert, one of the Military Staff of the President, and arranged that I should send them to him. I then got hold of a reliable man to take them, and asked the King's second valet to show them to him. He pointed out two large wooden packing-cases, and so having made sure that my instructions were quite clear, I went off to dress for dinner. I found a large number of Pressmen, photographers and various officials waiting to see me and had a very brisk time. Just as I was dressing the telephone in my bedroom rang, and I found it was Colonel Aldebert asking me whether he should have the boxes unpacked. I replied certainly he should, and proceeded to dress. Again the telephone went, and again it was Colonel Aldebert, who said he had found six busts of the King and Queen.

He added: '*Je me demande pourquoi six?*' I then realized that the King's valet had sent the wrong box. I hastily explained the whole thing to

★ Later Duke of Gloucester and Duke of Kent.

Colonel Aldebert and, having tumbled into my full dress uniform, I flew off and got hold of Howlett the valet. I was told by the footman that he was busy with the King's uniform. I replied that the matter was so serious that if he did not come at once there would be serious trouble. He soon after appeared with an aggrieved expression. He was usually so wonderful and businesslike that I was surprised at his making such a mistake, but I explained that I must have the right box at once. I got hold of the trusty Frenchman and explained that he was to take them at once to the Elysée and bring back the other two boxes. I just managed to give these instructions before the King and Queen appeared ready to drive off to dinner at the Elysée.

It would have become a huge joke in Paris if the King had by mistake presented six busts of himself and the Queen to the President. Luckily, however, all went well, and after the dinner the King in a short speech presented the medallions to the President. The dinner was bad at the Elysée, as they apparently had no idea of catering for two hundred; I sat between Madame Marcel Prévost and Madame de Lannay, the wife of the President du Conseil Municipal. The King read his speech remarkably well in French, but with a true British accent. After dinner we smoked, and then there was an entertainment which was charming.

★   ★   ★

In April 1921 Bonar Law and his daughter came to stay at Windsor Castle from Saturday to Monday. I knew him slightly and had once or twice played bridge with him. Although reserved and difficult to know, he became quite human when he thawed and had a great sense of humour. After his son was killed in the war he gave up going out into society and never went anywhere except to the House of Commons.

It was four years after his son's death when he came to Windsor and so he had more or less recovered from his grief.

On Sunday the King said to me that he and the Queen were motoring to see somebody, and I was therefore to find out what Bonar Law would like to do and make the necessary arrangements. I asked Bonar Law to say frankly what he would like most to do. Would he like to go round the pictures and furniture? But he said this would bore him. I then suggested the library, but he said that he would want a week at least to see this even superficially. He would rather go out. I suggested the farms, but he said this would be worse than the pictures. After I had exhausted all the usual sights with no success, I said he had better propose something himself. He said he would like to go for a drive in the park with his daughter, and I replied that nothing would be easier.

I asked whether he would care to play bridge when he returned, but he said he had quite given up cards, and added that what he would really like was a game of chess. He warned me, however, that it was no use asking him to play 'bumble-puppy' chess, as that was tiresome. He had of late years studied chess very thoroughly and now invariably played with professionals, but of course he could not expect anything of this sort at Windsor; all he asked was someone who could play a first-class game. I said I quite understood and would arrange all this.

I went away and ordered the carriage, but scratched my head over the chess. My own chess was infantile and therefore out of the question, and although I knew that some of the Household played chess, I was quite sure that their games came under the head of 'bumble-puppy' and that it was a waste of time to ask them to take on Bonar Law. It suddenly occurred to me that Sir Walter Parratt had in his day been a first-rate player, and that I remembered his telling me that he found all the chess problems in the newspapers never took him more than ten minutes to solve.

So I wrote a note to him asking him to come and play Bonar Law at chess soon after six; that is, after the evening service at St George's Chapel. Then a short scribble to Bonar Law explaining who Parratt was. When I thought I had arranged everything I found there was some difficulty about the board and chessmen. There were innumerable and valuable sets under glass cases, but a common or garden board seemed impossible to find. I consulted Derek Keppel, the Master of the Household, and he at once started his myrmidons on the scent of one. Eventually, an ordinary set was found in the cupboard of the room that was formerly where Princess Mary worked with her governess.

Keppel arranged a charming setting for the game with a small table, two comfortable arm-chairs and shaded electric light lamps.

I went to the room soon after six and talked to Bonar Law. When Parratt came in I introduced them, and while a footman handed cigars and offered tea or coffee, Bonar Law whispered in my ear: 'Isn't my opponent a bit old?' I merely replied that he knew the game; as a matter of fact, Parratt was eighty or more. So I left them.

I heard afterwards that they played in dead silence for an hour and that Parratt then said: '*That* is checkmate.' Bonar Law replied: 'Not at all, I have seven different moves.' 'Precisely,' said Parratt, 'but if you move one, I do so and so. Checkmate. If you move two, I do so and so; again checkmate.' He went through the whole seven moves and described what would happen in each case.

Bonar Law studied this for twenty minutes and then said: 'That is right.' I told the King and, not very tactfully, when His Majesty came to dinner he said to Bonar Law: 'I hear old Parratt beat your head off at chess.' Bonar Law merely said he had had a very interesting game.

Poor Charles Cust's death in 1931 was a great blow to the King and all the Household felt the loss. His great charm was that he was so offensively rude to people he didn't like, and when therefore his face lit up and his blue eyes sparkled when he met one, there was no doubt at all that he was pleased. The impostor, the swaggerer, were his particular 'bêtes noires' and he never made any attempt to conceal his dislike. Curiously, the rabbit type he was always kind to, and he generally found in such men unexpected qualities quite alien to their rodent nature. Little children delighted him and flocked to him naturally, while many grown-ups approached him with utmost caution. To the King he was invaluable; he never hesitated to speak his mind bluntly and even brutally, but His Majesty knew him so well that he never minded even being flatly contradicted by him. I remember soon after the King had ascended the throne, Cust was seated in the billiards-room at Balmoral looking at books from the London and Times Libraries, which he had piled on the floor in front of him. The King came in and said: 'I say, Charles, is that the way you treat my books?'

Cust replied: '*Your* books! Why, you haven't in the whole of this house got a book that's worth reading. Your so-called library is nothing but beautifully bound piffle.'

Later, the King repeated this to me and asked me whether it was true. I told him that this was an accurate description of the library; it had been the practice during both Queen Victoria's and King Edward's reigns to put there presentation books which were usually quite unreadable, the best ones having been sent to the library at Windsor. His Majesty said he had not had time to look at the books in the library, but if this was the case a certain sum every year should be devoted to the purchase of interesting Scottish books and the worthless ones should be weeded out.

The Fatal Gun, 1872

(Concerning the relationship of Fritz Ponsonby's father, Sir Henry Ponsonby, with Queen Victoria, to whom he was Private Secretary)

Queen Victoria had little love for London: she disliked its noise, its fogs, its fierce unbridled materialism. By contrast she loved the moors and braes of Balmoral, the sunny freshness of Osborne, and even the dignified feudalism of Windsor, where she held many state functions. But where Windsor could be reached easily by train and almost by carriage drive, and Balmoral by a comfortable railway journey, Osborne, in the Isle of Wight, required a short sea trip. For this purpose Queen Victoria used the second largest of the two Royal yachts, the *Alberta*, while the smallest, the *Elfin*, was utilized to carry messengers, members of the Household and officials whose social standing was not high enough to entitle them to use the *Alberta*. The largest Royal yacht, the *Victoria & Albert*, a dignified paddle-wheel steamer picked out in black and gold, with deck cabins of gleaming white and funnels of light buff, was intended for Queen Victoria's more public appearances at sea, for naval reviews, Royal welcomes, etc., but as a matter of fact she was very seldom used.

In 1872 there were held the usual manoeuvres of the Channel Fleet. The Queen never attended them, but it was agreed that the Prince of Wales (later Edward VII) should represent her and should utilize the *Victoria & Albert*, whose captain, Prince Leiningen, was a half-nephew of Queen Victoria by the Duchess of Kent's first marriage. The presence of the Royal yacht at manoeuvres was quite an innovation, and a precedent – that stronghold of the red-tape mind – did not exist regarding its function or position.

According to the usual naval routine an evening gun is fired every day by the officer in command of the fleet. This firing of the gun is not a simple ceremony: it indicates to the assembled fleet who is the Senior Flag Officer, where he is to be found, and where to look for orders. It also gives the time to the fleet or squadron, denotes the setting of the watch and the time for placing the guard boats and look-outs. Similarly, the morning, or daylight gun, sanctions the relief of the watch and look-outs, and is the signal for the recall of the guard boats. Thus the gun signal was of no little importance.

It was on the 10th of August 1872 that the firing of this gun caused such an explosion that its reverberations made even the Cabinet shake in their shoes, for it was fired, not at the order of Rear-Admiral Hornby, who was in command of the Channel Fleet; nor of Admiral Sir Sydney Dacres, the First Sea Lord, who was there for the manoeuvres; nor even of Mr Goschen, the First Lord of the Admiralty, but at the order of that very junior captain, Prince Leiningen. Worse still, it was fired a few seconds too early, as if to emphasize his right to fire the gun.

At the moment, Admiral Sir Sydney Dacres was on board the Royal yacht. The outrageous conduct of Prince Leiningen he considered to be so serious that, instead of remonstrating with him verbally, he sat down in his cabin and indited the following semi-official letter:

> My dear Prince Leiningen – I beg leave to inform you, to avoid mistakes, that the Daylight Gun tomorrow morning will be fired by the *Minotaur* bearing the flag of the officer commanding the Channel Fleet. I am quite sure you must be well aware that the yacht firing an evening and morning gun is quite an innovation under present circumstances, more particularly when the Admiralty had informed Rear-Admiral Hornby that he was to conduct the duties of the fleet in the usual manner. I think I may frankly say that the Admiralty are much surprised at having a gun fired from the Royal yacht as they are quite unaware of any regulation of the Service that would authorize it, and they see how very much inconvenience would attend on such a departure from custom.
>
> Yours sincerely,
>
> S. Dacres.

Prince Leiningen, being only a captain, had to be careful in what he said to so exalted a personage as the First Sea Lord, and his reply, delivered a few minutes later, ran:

> Dear Sir Sydney Dacres – I am excessively sorry you should think I had done anything unusual in firing a gun at 9 o'clock. It has *always* been the custom to do so ever since I have been in the yacht when the Royal Standard is flying. An

instance of this occurred only five months ago in Portsmouth harbour, and I am sure Sir Rodney Mundy★ himself will bear me out in what I say.

Believe me to remain, Very sincerely yours,

Leiningen.

I shall be much obliged to you [he added] if you kindly will let me know your decision on the matter in question, so that I may know what to do tomorrow morning.

Sir Sydney Dacres, as he sat in his cabin, must have been relieved to find that the incident had ended so satisfactorily. He had kept up his end and successfully remonstrated with Prince Leiningen. He could, therefore, unbend a little since there was now no prospect of paper warfare; so he wrote this time to 'My Dear Leiningen' a letter which he thought would close the whole incident.

In answer to your note [his reply ran] the precedent you quote at Portsmouth is not a point. The Queen was on board, and if I may quote my own experience, it was then a novelty. But here we have a large fleet – the Admiralty themselves are present, and the question is one far more of responsibility than ceremony – and nothing must be done to lessen the authority of those who are held responsible. Rear-Admiral Hornby must therefore, as has been ordered, fire the gun.

Yours sincerely,

S. Dacres.

The Queen's Regulations [he added as a postscript] confine the firing of a gun to flag officers and commodores. (See Page 2. Article 10.)

The marine orderly who was acting as messenger, having had a busy evening taking letters from one cabin to another, was now to spend a restless night. First of all Sir Sydney Dacres thought it prudent to send an account of the incident to the First Lord of the Admiralty on board the *Enchantress*, together with copies of the letters that had passed between him and Prince Leiningen. Then there must have been a conference on the *Victoria & Albert* between the Prince of Wales, Prince Leiningen and Colonel Grey (father of Viscount Grey of Fallodon), at which the decision was reached that Prince Leiningen should continue to fire the gun.

The marine orderly, having already delivered Sir Sydney Dacres' packet of letters, had therefore to go a second time to the *Enchantress*, this time from the *Victoria & Albert*, with the following letter for Mr Goschen, the First Lord of the Admiralty:

Sir – I am desired by His Royal Highness the Prince of Wales to inform you that

★ Commander-in-Chief at Portsmouth.

Prince Leiningen has placed the correspondence between Sir S. Dacres and himself in His Royal Highness' hands, and as His Royal Highness' Standard is flying on board the Royal yacht, and as moreover His Royal Highness is here as the Queen's representative, he has ordered Prince Leiningen to fire the morning and evening gun according to the usual custom of the Royal yachts.

I have the honour to be, Sir, Your obedient Servant,

G. Grey,
Equerry-in-Waiting.

The question was now posed for Mr Goschen to answer. He, as First Lord of the Admiralty, represented the Government as the civilian head of the Navy. He, or his predecessor, had been responsible for appointing Rear-Admiral Hornby to the command of the Channel Fleet, and could therefore delegate to him the duty of firing the gun. But the Prince of Wales was there as heir-apparent, representing the Queen, and furthermore quite determined to exercise all Royal privilege. Naval manoeuvres were Greek to Mr Goschen, who was enjoying a pleasant sea holiday at the Government's expense, but constitutional precedents he felt to be his own particular territorial waters.

Colonel Grey's letter reached the *Enchantress* at 2 a.m., but no one dared disturb a sleeping First Lord, and seven o'clock came, the time for the firing of the day-light gun, before the civilian 'ruler of the Queen's Navee' had had his morning cup of tea or the morning's mail. Meanwhile, the Prince of Wales had given orders to Prince Leiningen to fire the gun from the *Victoria & Albert*, while Sir Sydney Dacres had sent similar instructions to Admiral Hornby to fire it from the flagship. Suddenly the placid morning air of the Solent was rent by two explosions – two morning guns had been fired! They awoke Mr Goschen, who probably wondered what all the row was about. A few minutes later he opened Sir Sydney Dacres' and Colonel Grey's letters and realized that something unpleasant had happened; what it was exactly he was unable for the moment to grasp. Breakfast was soon despatched and he hurriedly summoned to a consultation the Sea Lords and Admiralty officials, whose apoplectic countenances made it clear that he was expected to take a very serious view of the matter.

The consultation resulted in so bewildering Mr Goschen that he decided to lay the whole matter before Queen Victoria, and his letter to her, dated August 11, ran:

Mr Goschen presents his humble duty to Your Majesty and much regrets to feel it incumbent upon him to lay before Your Majesty the following particulars of an incident which occurred yesterday evening in connection with the Royal yacht.

What is technically called 'the evening gun' was fired from the *Victoria & Albert* by Captain His Serene Highness Prince Leiningen, under what the Admiralty believes to be a misapprehension of the regulations known as 'The Queen's Regulations for the Government of Her Majesty's Naval Service'. Under these regulations the right of firing a gun on certain occasions is limited to Flag Officers and Commodores, and when more than one are present, the senior only can exercise the right (Mr Goschen encloses the words of this regulation in question). Consequently the firing of the gun is not a simple ceremony. It indicates to the assembled vessels who is the Senior Flag Officer present and therefore in command.

The Lords of the Admiralty, being officially present in Portland and having had delegated to them by Your Majesty's gracious commission the supreme authority over Your Majesty's Naval Forces, had directed Rear-Admiral Hornby, the Commander-in-Chief of the Channel Squadron, to carry on the duties of Commander-in-Chief during their stay at Portland.

The Lords of the Admiralty were distinctly of opinion that it was Rear-Admiral Hornby who, under the regulations, was alone entitled to fire the evening gun, and that the step taken by the captain of the Royal yacht was contrary to the regulation. Had there been a question of ceremony, no difficulty whatever would have been raised, but the important point involved was who was entitled to command of the fleet assembled.

It was thought that H.S.H. Prince Leiningen had acted under a mistake, and Admiral Sir Sydney Dacres, the Senior Naval Lord, pointed this out to him in writing. Prince Leiningen in reply pointed to a precedent which he believed to be applicable, and asked to be informed of Sir Sydney Dacres' decision so as to guide him with reference to the morning gun. Sir Sydney Dacres then informed Prince Leiningen that the precedent did not apply as Your Majesty had been present in person on the occasion in question, and that the morning gun would be fired by Admiral Hornby. Mr Goschen begs to add that as the regulation prescribes that only Flag Officers should fire these guns from their ships it was not known to the Lords of the Admiralty that they had been fired from the Royal yacht.

Mr Goschen most humbly ventures to point out to Your Majesty that it is a very serious question in every point of view under what circumstances the supreme command over ships of war (and the consequent responsibilities) should be exercised by any of those to whom Your Majesty had delegated it by Royal Commission, and that the flying of the Royal Standard on any ship, especially if Your Majesty is not on board in person, cannot in itself be held to derogate from that delegated power, or to transfer it to any other quarter.

Mr Goschen should add that the letters of Sir Sydney Dacres were written to Prince Leiningen·in his capacity of a Naval officer on questions arising out of the Queen's Regulations, and that the Lords of the Admiralty had no information as to any personal intervention in the matter.

After the last letter of Sir Sydney Dacres to Prince Leiningen, His Royal Highness the Prince of Wales caused Mr Goschen to be informed that he had given an order (as the representative of Your Majesty) that the gun should be fired from the Royal yacht, but Mr Goschen, deeply as he regrets that any such question should have been raised between His Royal Highness and the Admiralty, feels bound to point out that in his humble opinion His Royal Highness the Prince of Wales did not obtain authority over the ships of war present by the fact of the Royal Standard flying on the yacht, or by being deputed by Your Majesty to act as her representative on the occasion of a ceremonial. Mr Goschen humbly hopes that Your Majesty will pardon him for placing this matter before Your Majesty. The point at the moment might be considered of less importance if it did not carry with it ulterior questions, as to the authority of members of the Royal Family over Your Majesty's Forces on other occasions.

The letter written to Mr Goschen by command of the Prince of Wales, of which he encloses a copy, was not brought to him till seven o'clock this morning, though it was brought on board the *Enchantress* at two in the night. Had Mr Goschen had any notice of His Royal Highness' personal intervention in this case, Mr Goschen would have at once asked permission to wait on His Royal Highness and to explain to him the difficulties of the position. As it was, Rear-Admiral Hornby fired the morning gun in accordance with the notice which had been sent to Prince Leiningen, and the latter also fired the gun, possibly in consequence of no reply having arrived to the letter sent to Mr Goschen by His Royal Highness' command, but which did not reach him till the gun had been fired.

Mr Goschen need scarcely assure Your Majesty that he deeply laments any annoyance which may have been caused to His Royal Highness in the course of proceedings in which His Royal Highness had graciously consented to take part.

Mr Goschen still desires to mention for the information of Your Majesty that the Standard flying on the *Victoria & Albert* was that of H.R.H. the Prince of Wales, though Mr Goschen had spoken of it in this letter simply as the Royal Standard.

The Queen received Mr Goschen's letter just before breakfast on the morning of the 12th August, and with it the following explanatory memorandum which had been prepared for her by the Naval Secretary at the Admiralty:

Memorandum

The firing of the evening gun in any port or roadstead denotes the presence of the flag officer in command of a fleet or squadron, to whom, during the night, the several commanding officers will look for instructions by signal in any emergencies which may arise.

It is accompanied by the hoisting by the flag officer of the top light and the uncovering of the stern lights, which are invariably shown at sea and in harbour or roadstead in addition to the position light on the fore stay.

It also gives the time to the squadron, and denotes the setting of the watch, the rowing of guards and placing look-outs.

The firing of the morning gun in like manner denotes daylight and sanctions the relief of the look-outs and watch who in war-time are kept at their guns or under arms on the quarter-deck in readiness for immediate action, and it is also the signal for the recall of the guard boats.

The words used in the Queen's Regulations and Admiralty instructions clearly indicate that the firing of the gun is left to the discretion and judgement of the Admiral in Command.

In war-time it might frequently be considered inexpedient to fire the gun as it might apprise a watchful enemy, not only of the position of a fleet or squadron, but it would also denote that the force was sufficient to be under the command of an admiral or commander.

In war-time, moreover, the daylight gun is not fired by the officer commanding the fleet until by careful observation it has been ascertained that no approach of the enemy has been made under cover of the darkness and that the watch may be safely relieved.

The above considerations lead to the conclusion that the firing of the evening and morning gun is a token of the command exercised by an admiral or other officer responsible for the charge and duties of a fleet or squadron, that it is a military observance, and could not be set aside without impairing the authority of the admirals, and departing from the regulations and usages of the service founded on long experience.

The point in dispute had now been magnified into a big constitutional problem. The question who should fire a gun seemed so trivial that it could with a little common sense have been decided on the spot, but when it became symbolic of the rights of the Lords of the Admiralty, and when the Queen's supremacy at sea was questioned, it seemed a serious matter.

Queen Victoria asked her private secretary, Colonel H. Ponsonby, to draw up a memorandum on the subject, and his opinion was as follows:

The Admiralty question must be separated into several heads:

(1) The question of the Queen's supremacy at sea. I scarcely think this will be disputed. William IV by an Order in Council in 1833 directed that when the Sovereign was on board any vessel of war, the Royal Standard, the flag of the Lord High Admiral and the Union Jack should be displayed. Now I conceive that this implies the Sovereign and the minister are both on board and that all orders emanating from that ship are law to the Navy.

As to compliments, when these flags are flown all honours are paid from all ships and forts. But it is ordered in the Queen's Regulations that when the Royal Standard alone is flying, ships salute but forts do not – thereby implying there is a difference. The Prince's Standard is treated with the same respect as the Royal Standard.

I think, therefore, that no contention can be raised as to the Queen's right at sea, and that on this point the reply will chiefly be addressed to the remark made in the Queen's letter on the ignorance of the Admiralty respecting the custom which has been invariably observed.

If they admit the Queen's supremacy they cannot of course object to the

Queen's right to order the gun to be fired from the yacht, but they will deny that the custom was known. It has been so seldom put in force that only one well-authenticated case can be proved before this year, and the custom can of course only be invariable since the time the yacht has had guns on board.

This, however, would only be a sort of remonstrance against the charge brought against the Admiralty of ignorance of custom. I repeat I do not think they desire to dispute the Queen's undoubted supremacy.

(2) The position held by the Prince of Wales at Portland has been defined as representing the Sovereign. But in what way he represented the Queen is not so clear. It may be agreed that he was entitled to all the compliments paid to the Sovereign, but he held no warrant, nor was there any public notification of his so representing her, nor was it probable that the Queen intended to invest him with any power whatever. At any rate, he appears with his own standard flying, so that no announcement was made to the fleet that he was anything more than the Prince of Wales, entitled hereby to every honour and respect from the ships but invested with no command or responsibility.

Would it not be advisable that on public occasions when any of the princes represent the Queen, a notice to this effect should be made known?

The Prince, on this occasion, flew his own standard, which was entitled by the regulation to the same compliments as the Royal Standard, but not the same as the Royal Standard and the other two conjoined.

(3) The Admiralty, having received the Queen's warrant to command the Navy, refuse to admit the right of any other person to command the Navy without a similar warrant from the Queen. There cannot, of course, be two commanders. Therefore, while according all respect and honour to the Prince of Wales, they steadfastly maintain the right as derived from the Queen to command the Navy, and no one else.

They cannot allow the Queen's warrant to them to be disputed.

The Admiralty only could command the fleet at Portland. They alone, without any other order, ordered the fleet to Portland, and ordered the fleet away. Without touching the question of courtesy, they maintain as a right that they had the right to order all the ships away while the Prince was there. Of course, this is pushing the question to the extreme, but they are most firm on the rights which belong to them by the Constitution. This being so, they consider that any order given by the Prince of Wales was an infringement of their rights. Either he or they must have the power. They maintain that they have, and therefore that the order given by H.R.H. that the gun should be fired was unconstitutional.

(4) On writing to Prince Leiningen the Admiralty received a reply from him in which, after touching on the above-mentioned subject, he asserted a claim which they entirely deny. They evidently lay great stress on this point, and he does so equally. He claims the right of the Royal yacht – with the Royal Standard flying – to be Senior Officer. Therefore, whenever the Royal Standard is hoisted on board the *Victoria & Albert*, all commands issuing therefrom must be obeyed. The Admiralty emphatically deny such right, and deny also that the Royal yacht is entitled as a ship to any precedence over any other ship, except by reason of the flag it may display.

And the rules as to these flags being already stated, it does not appear that any special claim can be put forward on behalf of the Royal Standard alone to exercise command.

Henry F. Ponsonby.

Colonel Ponsonby thus tactfully gave it as his opinion that the Prince of Wales and Prince Leiningen were in the wrong, and this opinion he expressed even more frankly in a letter to his wife written that day from Osborne (August 12, 1872); in fact he averred that their action was 'subversive of discipline' and 'a direct incitement to mutiny':

In the afternoon Otho Fitzgerald★ came to see me. He apologized for interfering in a matter in which he really had no business, but said he felt this naval question might really lead to something serious, and he was anxious to let me know the feelings of the admirals. They were unanimous in affirming that the conduct of the Prince of Wales was so utterly subversive of discipline that he would not be surprised if the Admiralty Lords resigned if they were not supported. Leiningen had been ordered by the Lords of the Admiralty not to fire the gun. He had done so and was guilty of insubordination, for which some wished to try him by court-martial. 'But,' I said, 'all the Navy don't agree with you.' 'Ah,' said Otho, 'I know you mean Rim Macdonald [a retired admiral] and others. The Prince went round the fleet canvassing officers to take part in his view and secured Rim and one or two others. He has foolishly given their names. This is a direct incitation to mutiny, and no authorities can allow such a proceeding. The Prince, by ordering officers to disobey the Lords of the Admiralty to whom the Queen has delegated her power, has committed a grave act, and if the Queen supports him she gives these lords a snub they cannot stand. Goschen will stand or fall with them.' All this, of course, was discussed at length and I could not well make head, so I changed to my strong point. 'Do you mean to tell me that Goschen supports the junior lords who tell the Queen she has no right to fire this gun, that she was under a misapprehension in having ordered it, and that the practice was an innovation.'

I must say Otho stuck well up even for this – saying that command and responsibility must go together, and that the Queen, having confided the Navy to the care of the lords, could not withdraw it capriciously. He also maintained it was an innovation. He then turned back to his strong ground, the Portland affair, and said it had been grossly mismanaged, and that Leiningen had given the Prince bad advice. 'Well,' I said, 'that is hard on Leiningen.' 'If he didn't,' replied Otho, 'who did advise him? Was it his Privy Council consisting of Charles Beresford, Clonmel and Arthur Sumner? If he represents the Queen, who represents the Queen's advisers? It is absurd to say that the Navy is to obey the caprices of a Prince advised by a German prince and a knot of gay, giddy boys.' I felt unpleasant and so got back to Dacres, and Otho persisted in getting back to the Portland row. He ended by entreating me that no hurried action should be taken

★ Lord Otho Fitzgerald, brother of the Duke of Leinster, and a retired naval captain.

as consequences might be serious. Bids,* in the meanwhile, had written a letter for the Queen, very strong. I suggested moderation because: first, are we sure of our facts that the Queen has always fired this gun? second, had we better not fight solely the Queen's right? and third, above all things don't let us advance to any position which we should have to retire from with shame. Bids thereupon said he would keep the answer till tomorrow. But he says he won't allow the Queen to sacrifice any right. I quite agree, but we must clearly see it is a right. Cowell† won't listen to any doubt about the Queen's right, and says any question of it is legal quibbling, but, on the other hand, he thinks the Prince of Wales quite wrong. He says that flags are everything. The Prince exhibited his own flag alone, which (for all purposes of compliment only) is entitled to be treated as the Queen's Standard. His advice is throw the Prince over and maintain the Queen's right. Now, throwing the Prince over is a serious matter, and if we abandon that point the Admiralty will follow up their victory by insisting on their demands about the Queen. I seek for some mode of an amicable settlement, but don't see it yet. I lay awake half the night. I think the Queen should take a judicial tone, something like this: 'You, Goschen, complain to me of the Prince of Wales. You, Prince of Wales, complain to me of Goschen. You say you did so because I did, and you, Goschen, say I was wrong when I did so. Let us clear that up first.' But in any case I don't want the Queen to enter into controversy if it can be avoided, but to be above it. Besides, we can't fight from Scotland.

How tired you will be of all this, but it is a small thing that if not carefully judged may swell into a large one, so that it requires most careful handling. Of course, if I were the Queen I would send for Goschen and have it out with him. But that cannot be.

Queen Victoria, on receiving Mr Goschen's letter, must at first have thought it was merely a trivial matter relating to naval etiquette. The fact that her son had come to loggerheads with the Admiralty left her singularly cold, but when she read Colonel Ponsonby's memorandum and found that her supremacy at sea was being disputed, she at once plunged into the fray. Without going into the niceties of the technical arguments and the interpretation of the nebulous regulations, she put the controversy on a higher plane and wrote to Mr Goschen from Osborne on August 13:

Osborne,
August 13th, 1872.

The Queen has received Mr Goschen's letter respecting the misunderstanding which occurred at Portland, and has also seen copies of the correspondence which took place between Sir S. Dacres and Prince Leiningen and a letter from the Prince of Wales' equerry.

* General Sir Thomas Biddulph, Keeper of the Privy Purse to Queen Victoria.
† Sir John Cowell, Master of the Queen's Household.

The circumstances have given the Queen considerable annoyance, particularly as it appears to her that great misapprehension exists in the Board of Admiralty as to the custom of the Service with regard to her position, when on board the Royal yacht with the Royal Standard flying.

In his second letter to Prince Leiningen Sir S. Dacres observes, in reply to Prince Leiningen's observation that he had always fired the gun when on board the Royal yacht with the Royal Standard flying and once within a few months at Portsmouth, that, quoting his own (Sir S. Dacres') experience, such a proceeding was then a novelty, though the Queen was on board. Mr Goschen also observes that it was not known to the Lords of the Admiralty that such was the custom.

The Queen must express her surprise at this. The custom has been invariable during the Queen's reign, and she has no intention of dispensing with the mark of respect to the Sovereign which it indicates.

The Prince of Wales' (and the Prince Consort's) Standards are entitled by a special order to the same respect as the Queen's, and the Queen thinks, on the occasion of his visiting Portland as her representative, every respect should have been shown to him. No command or interference with the fleet is intended, but the Sovereign and the Prince of Wales can hardly be placed in the position of a private person on board, so that the ships of a squadron or fleet, accompanying the Royal yacht, might leave the harbour without announcing their intention to do so.

The Queen by no means desires, nor would she allow, the Prince of Wales to introduce any alteration in the regulations of the Service on these points. Nothing can be further from her wish than to deprive the Board of Admiralty of the authority they should exercise. All the Queen desires is to maintain the proper dignity of the Sovereign, or of the Heir Apparent representing her, and not to allow innovations to be introduced.

The circumstance of two morning guns having been fired appears to have arisen from misapprehension, owing to Mr Goschen not having received the letter addressed to him as intended, and the circumstances which led to it having occurred in the middle of the night, all personal communication was prevented, which, no doubt, would have removed the misunderstanding.

Victoria, R.

The Queen thus appeared to support the action of the Prince of Wales and Prince Leiningen. Mr Goschen, however, was determined not to let the matter rest here, and he instructed the Secretary of the Admiralty to call for a report of the incident from Prince Leiningen, whose report ran as follows (August 18):

Sir – In compliance with the request contained in your letter of the 17th inst., I have the honour to inform you:

(1) The morning and evening guns have not been fired since I have had command of the Royal yacht, with the Queen on board, except at Portsmouth in the month of March of the present year, both on leaving for and returning from Cherbourg.

Her Majesty has not stayed on board on any other occasions in the presence of a flag officer. A morning and evening gun was fired at Cherbourg in 1858 in the presence of both the Admiralty and Lord Lyons' squadron. I was then commander of the Royal yacht. The Admiralty flag was flying on board here on both occasions. A morning and evening gun was fired in 1868 at Kingstown (Ireland) with the Prince of Wales' Standard and no other flag flying. A flag officer (Rear-Admiral Warden) and a squadron was present at the time.

(2) No intimation has at any time been sent by me to any senior or flag officer of my intention to fire the gun, nor did I do so at Portland.

Ever since I have known the yacht, now nearly eighteen years, she has always been considered as senior officer in every case whenever the Royal Standard was flying with or without the Queen herself being on board.

(3) I did not inform the Commander-in-Chief at Portsmouth in March last of my intention to fire the gun. The Admiralty flag was flying on board here at that time, whilst at Portland it was not.

Then the matter simmered for over a month, ostensibly on account of the death of Princess Hohenlohe, but really because each side wanted time to strengthen their case.

But Colonel Ponsonby was determined to pour what oil he could on these troubled waters and suggested privately to Mr Goschen that, if the Portland incident could be dismissed as a misunderstanding, it would then only be necessary to discuss the new regulation that would obviate further trouble. His letter to Mr Goschen, written from Balmoral on September 26, runs:

The Queen inquired today about the memorandum and I said that you had not wished to trouble Her Majesty at the present moment with it.

As I had said I had spoken to you on the subject, the Queen expressed a hope that you did not intend to contest her undoubted right to supremacy afloat. I did not undertake to represent your views accurately, but repeating them to the best of my power assured her that I did not think you intended to question her rights and privileges, but only to explain that the infrequency of the custom of firing the gun at night from the Royal yacht justified the Admiralty in their ignorance that such was usual.

But if the Queen's supremacy is admitted the Admiralty should not have doubted her right to fire the gun.

The Regulations, however, are not so clear on this point as they might be, and the Queen thought that perhaps you would assure her of her rights and if necessary propose some addition to the Queen's Regulations that would put the matter beyond doubt.

I did not enter into the details of the question of the Prince of Wales beyond remarking that I felt sure I was not misrepresenting you in saying you thought the Queen's Regulations very obscure on that point also, and that, although you believed that Prince Leiningen was wrong both in what he did at Portland, and what he afterwards claimed on behalf of the yacht, you admitted there was ample room to allow of the misunderstanding.

Will not any controversy on this point in its present form assume to a certain extent a personal tone in so much as it may condemn the acts of individuals who may have considered themselves justified by custom and by portions of the Regulations?

If so, would it not be better that the incident at Portland should be considered entirely as a misunderstanding, and, being treated as such, be no further alluded to? – but that new rules founded on the case should be drawn up by you and submitted for the Queen's consideration – and that the discussion should then take place on the proposed rules?

This proposal is only mine, so that you are quite at liberty to reject it, and, at the same time, I should scarcely like you to accept it before I have consulted the Prince of Wales, but I have taken the liberty of suggesting this, as a cold and dry discussion of rules would, I think, be preferable to a hot controversy on the acts of individuals. – Yours very truly,

Henry Ponsonby.

The Prince of Wales, who was now at Abergeldie Castle, close to Balmoral, followed the discussion closely, and to Colonel Ponsonby he wrote on September 28:

Many thanks for sending me all the correspondence relative to the 'incident at Portland'. I should be very glad to have some conversation with you on the subject – perhaps the Queen would give you permission to lunch here tomorrow – so that I may speak to you afterwards.

Colonel Ponsonby thought it well to keep Prince Leiningen also informed about the proposal he had put forward to Mr Goschen.

It was unlucky [he wrote on September 28] that the illness and death of Princess Hohenlohe prevented Mr Goschen from communicating with the Queen on the Portland incident.

I cannot help thinking that there are innumerable difficulties in the case arising from the want of preciseness in the regulation and that the discussion as to what each individual did must degenerate into a personal dispute. I think it would be undesirable that the Queen and the Prince of Wales should be mixed up in anything that is personal, and I imagine that Your Serene Highness would much prefer that the argument should take place on the merits of the case.

The question of the Queen having supreme authority when she is afloat on any vessel of war with the Royal Standard, the flag of the Lord High Admiral and the Union Jack flying is, I imagine, beyond dispute, though it must be affirmed now more clearly.

I venture to suggest, therefore, whether it would not be as well that the Portland incident should be treated as a misunderstanding by all parties, and that no further discussion should take place on the acts of individuals on that occasion, but that new rules or amended regulations, founded on the necessity arising for such rules from the obscurity of those which exist, should be framed by the Admiralty and submitted to the Queen, and upon these a discussion may fairly take place. Do you think this would be advisable?

Mr Goschen, feeling that the Portland incident strengthened his hand, was loath to drop it. A cut-and-dried discussion on future regulations might place him in a difficult position and he might be forced to give way. On September 30, he wrote to Colonel Ponsonby:

You say: 'Would it not be better that the incident at Portland should be considered entirely as a misunderstanding, and being treated as such be no further alluded to.'

I quite concur in the desirability of treating the question in the abstract. But how does it stand now? That the Queen has written a very strong letter to me officially, in which the action of the Admiralty is strongly commented on. That letter I can, of course, scarcely treat as other than a letter directed to me officially in the character of the First Lord of the Admiralty. I cannot leave that letter unanswered or unexplained. It would be unjust to my colleagues and myself.

If the whole correspondence were withdrawn it would be a different matter, but I do not think it can possibly close with the last letter I have received. That letter cannot remain as the final record of the incident at Portland.

With regard to the other part of your letter, it is always a most difficult matter to report a long conversation to another person in a few sentences.

I admitted that the regulations as to the hoisting of the flag were not as clear as they might be, but I certainly did not intend to convey that any ambiguity in the Regulations afforded 'ample room to allow for the misunderstanding' as regards the action of Prince Leiningen when the Prince of Wales was on board – nor was there any ambiguity which in my judgement could justify the giving of an order by the Prince of Wales as to a matter connected with the fleet.

You appear to have misunderstood me to mean that while I thought Prince Leiningen was wrong there was great excuse for him on account of the Regulations. I was far from meaning that. The difficulty in the Regulations is with regard to the hoisting of the three flags, and what is the position of the Sovereign when the three flags are not hoisted, but only the Royal Standard? But that does not exculpate Prince Leiningen on the particular occasion in question. I think that the officers of the yacht have created some customs on a very narrow basis without the knowledge of the Admiralty, in the teeth of the Regulations. Then they plead these alleged customs against the Regulations, and the poor Regulations are then to be condemned.

I have delayed further action till I had really gathered all the facts together and I have now done so. As to your first suggestion, you will have understood what I mean. I should prefer a dry correspondence as to *future* rules and would most gladly hail a release from the necessity of dealing with the past, but so long as the last letter is in full force, you will agree with me that I have no alternative but to deal with the points it raises. – Yours very truly,

G. Goschen.

Prince Leiningen, who was a junior captain, while perfectly willing to support the Prince of Wales, did not like the idea of the Queen and the Admiralty deciding the larger issues in a spirit of amicability, while leaving him to be the scapegoat on the minor issues. He therefore wrote to Colonel Ponsonby on October 2:

> I quite agree with you that the discussion of the Portland business should not become a personal dispute and that, as you suggest, new regulations on the subject should be submitted to the Queen. Whatever decision is then arrived at will be a guidance for myself on future occasions. Moreover, it can be a matter of perfect indifference to me whether Her Majesty is pleased to give in to the Admiralty or not, which really and truly is the point at issue. I only have to obey and to do as I am told.
>
> But there is another side to the question, entirely separate from the 'Standard' business in itself. I mean the way my own case has been prejudged by their Lordships. I have been pitched into, privately, by Sir Sydney Dacres, and in his letter to the Queen, Mr Goschen very considerately tried to throw all the blame on me. Moreover, there has been a very nasty article in the *Army and Navy Gazette*, abusing myself, who, from being on full pay, am not allowed to open my mouth in self-defence.
>
> Now if, as you suggest, I drop the matter altogether, I admit myself snubbed, although 'right or wrong', I merely have carried out the routine of the yacht such as it is and has been for the last thirty years.
>
> Besides, people will say the matter has been hushed up because I am the Queen's nephew, etc., etc. I think, instead of being told on official foolscap that I ought to have known 'better', I have a right to expect a *letter* to say I have acted to the best of my judgement. That is the mildest way I can put it. – Sincerely yours,
> Leiningen.

As Leiningen indicated, the story leaked out and the 'very nasty article' of which he complained appeared in the *United Services Gazette* on September 28, 1872. It was a travesty of the incident in the form of a letter headed 'The Fatal Gun'.

Meanwhile Queen Victoria had no intention of following Mr Goschen's suggestion that she should withdraw her letter, and the Prince of Wales seemed opposed to the proposal to drop the Portland incident. There was, therefore, nothing to be done but to carry on the discussions. Consequently Colonel Ponsonby wrote to Mr Goschen on October 5:

> I am sorry I did not clearly comprehend your meaning about there being room for misunderstanding in the Portland incident.
>
> But I only repeated in very general terms to the Queen my impression of what I supposed to be your opinion. As the Queen is very tenacious of her rights at sea, and as her letter to you was almost entirely devoted to the assertion of her rights,

I scarcely think I could propose to her to withdraw that letter. I may as well mention to you that I spoke to the Prince of Wales and made my suggestion to him. He did not seem to think it was possible to obliterate the Portland incident for reasons which are too long to enter into here. But ultimately he seemed ready to listen to my proposal. As the matter at present stands you will, I suppose, send the Queen the memorandum you have prepared.

The suggestion I made was merely mine and its non-adoption simply leaves the question as it was.

Since the question might be referred to the Prime Minister, Mr Gladstone, and the Cabinet, Colonel Ponsonby took the precaution of enlisting the sympathies of Lord Halifax, the Lord Privy Seal, a member of the Cabinet and a *persona grata* with Queen Victoria, and while Lord Halifax liked the proposal to drop the Portland incident, he took a serious view of the Prince of Wales having given an order to an officer of the Navy. To Colonel Ponsonby he wrote on October 7:

I have read over your letter since I came here and I am quite sure that the first step which you suggest, *i.e.* treating what has happened at Portland as a *misunderstanding*, is the wisest and best course.

The Prince cannot really suppose that Sir S. Dacres was *intentionally* guilty of disrespect. Mr Goschen cannot suppose that P. Leiningen committed an act of insubordination. Captain Tryon, Mr Goschen's private secretary, whom I met at Drummond Castle, seems to me to be of this opinion, though it is fair to say that whilst he knew all about it, I do not know that he represented Mr Goschen's opinion.

I will not now enter into the question of the Queen herself being on board the yacht. It does not arise here, and we should only complicate the present matter by going into it.

I hold it to be indisputable that the Prince of Wales can give no orders to any public officer in the administration of public affairs.

He has no authority of his own – he can only derive it from the Queen.

It is impossible to say, when he goes down to act for the Queen in a matter of ceremony, that this gives him authority over any part of the administration of public departments.

Certain persons are entrusted with the performance of certain duties and functions by formal commission, patent or authority from the Queen, and such authority cannot be superseded except by similar authority as formally conveyed.

It is essentially for the interest of the Sovereign that this should be so. If any public official was bound to obey a Prince who could show no formal authority from the Sovereign, it would in old times have gone far to warrant officers in aiding rebellion by an undutiful son.

I am going up to a Cabinet to be held on Thursday, and I will speak to Mr Goschen on the subject.

Yours truly,

Halifax.

The whole question was now before the Cabinet, of which Mr Gladstone was the head, and of which Lord Halifax, as Lord Privy Seal, was one of the most important members. The task of explaining to an apathetic and possibly soporific Cabinet the enormity of the crime that had been committed by the Prince of Wales and the implied insults that had been levelled at my Lords of the Admiralty must have taxed Mr Goschen's powers to the utmost. Possibly he may have made some impression on a few Cabinet Ministers who were not too much occupied with their own departmental affairs to listen to him, but he appears to have made little impression on Mr Gladstone who only wanted to settle the matter in a manner that would satisfy Queen Victoria. It must have been pure Greek to Mr Gladstone, and probably the other Cabinet Ministers were totally unable to understand what the controversy was about, but Mr Goschen had to support the Lords of the Admiralty and make their point of view clear to the Cabinet. A few minutes before the meeting (October 14) Lord Halifax wrote to Colonel Ponsonby:

Dear Ponsonby – We have been so busy that I have not been able to see Mr Goschen till this morning, and here I am in the Cabinet room with the Cabinet meeting to take place in five minutes, so I have no time to write to you today.

There is no hurry and there are one or two matters to be looked into, and whatever is done should be done thoroughly. – Yours truly,

Halifax.

A few days after the Cabinet meeting, Lord Halifax raised the whole constitutional point again, and even suggested that the Queen should relinquish her right of precedence at sea. To this Colonel Ponsonby replied on October 24, 1872:

Dear Lord Halifax – I was very sorry to get your letter disputing what I had understood to be beyond dispute.

I sincerely hope you will not ask me to submit it to the Queen, as I feel it would not help us to a quiet solution.

You ask that the Queen should withdraw her letter and that she should relinquish her right of precedence at sea.

When I privately inquired if the past could be forgotten I was reminded that the Queen's letter was the last recorded, and that it would not be just to the Admiralty that it should remain unanswered. I quite saw the truth of this argument, and I cannot conceive now why the Queen is to withdraw her letter and leave as the last recorded document the complaint of the Admiralty and the accusation brought against the Queen by the First Naval Lord that Her Majesty had been guilty of introducing an unauthorized innovation. Surely you would not advise the Queen to take no notice of this. As to the point itself, it is a question of fact whether it was correct or not, and I think you will find the custom has been sanctioned by the Lords of the Admiralty. You ask me what I mean by the Queen's supremacy and what Prince Leiningen means. I cannot say what Prince Leiningen means for I have never spoken to him on this part of the question, and have only seen that part of his letter which Mr Goschen showed me. What I mean by supremacy is entire precedence in command, honour and dignity. You ask if the Sovereign sent away a ship that was wrecked, would he not be responsible. I cannot conceive such a case, for a sovereign who exercised his power in this way would soon cease to be a sovereign. If you push arguments to absurdity, I would ask whether you mean that an admiral could order off the Royal yacht at any moment. These are straining the Constitution and must snap the delicately arranged machine. But the form of command, it seems to me, must belong to the Queen, for you would never advise she should be under some admiral.

Mr Goschen asked me if a Royal Standard alone could be considered equal to the Royal Standard and two other flags. No more can the Admiralty flying a jack be equal to all three. The Standard and an Admiralty flag conjoined imply the Queen is there with the Lords of the Admiralty. G. will say this is a fiction, but not more so than hundreds of fictions in everyday life and in our Constitution.

I have asked First Lord to look at the papers and should be glad of some mode of settling the difficult question, but I do really think that your proposal would light up a flame and not allay one.

You say there would be no difficulty in firing the gun, but it was the difficulty of firing the gun that raised this controversy.

Two days later (October 26) Colonel Ponsonby wrote to Mrs Ponsonby:

I sat up some time writing on Thursday and considering whether I should send Lord Halifax the semi-chaff letter in which under cover of chaff I could say a great deal, or the serious letter which you thought was treating the subject too much *au sérieux*. But I thought the chaff might offend, and I thought also it was as well he should know that the Queen will be pretty determined if he demands she shall withdraw the letter of censure on the Admiralty for not knowing she always has fired the gun – as she has – and that she shall give up her privilege at sea. So I sent the stiff letter. Of course if it came to a fight it must end in her giving up these rights, but it will be a very ugly thing for the Government to demand, placed in the light it has been done. And Forster★ will certainly not join in doing anything that has the appearance of discourtesy.

Mr Goschen now took up the argument again, and with almost exaggerated deference wrote to the Queen on December 9, 1872, and made it clear that nothing was further from the thoughts of the Lords of the Admiralty than any want of respect either to her or to the Prince of Wales, but he politely insisted that the gun must be fired from the

★ Generally thought to be the probable successor to Mr Gladstone should he retire.

flagship. Therefore the only solution he could suggest was that a gun should be fired from both the Royal yacht and the flagship, the latter taking time by the former.

The peacemaker, Lord Halifax, was pleased his efforts were now bearing fruit, and on December 19, 1872, wrote to Colonel Ponsonby:

Dear Ponsonby – I am very glad indeed to get your letter, and to see the prospect of a solution *à l'amiable* of the Portland affair. I told Mr Goschen you and I had agreed on the wisest thing being to consider all that passed at Portland as *non avenu* – and he quite agreed.

If the Prince of Wales concurs, then the most awkward part of the business is got rid of.

Nobody ever dreamt of putting the Queen under the order of the Admiral, and as to the ceremony of firing the gun, it ought to be provided for in the Queen's Regulations, and there need be no difficulty about it.

Queen Victoria didn't seem to mind how many guns were fired, or where they were fired, so long as the Royal yacht fired one first, and her letter to Mr Goschen, on January 3, 1873, bears the truly regal imprint:

The Queen has given due consideration to Mr Goschen's letter of the 9th ult., in reply to hers of August last, respecting an incident which occurred when the Royal yacht with the Prince of Wales on board was in the harbour off Portland.

The Queen is willing to accept Mr Goschen's explanation that no intention existed of treating the Prince of Wales with disrespect, and desires to pass over that circumstance, and is also willing to believe that the Lords of the Admiralty present on that occasion were unaware of the custom, which has for so long a time prevailed, of the evening and morning gun being fired from the Royal yacht when the Royal Standard is flying. Still, the custom has prevailed, and the Queen believes no instance of the non-observance of it can be found. Mr Goschen observes that Prince Leiningen can only state two instances, in 1858 and 1872. These will be found to be the only occasions since 1857 when the Queen has remained on board at night in the presence of an admiral. In 1858 the Board of Admiralty were also present. The Queen has no objection to a regulation being inserted that when she is on board the gun shall be fired from the Royal yacht, or other ship on which the Royal Standard is hoisted, and that the Flag Officer present may follow the firing of the gun . . . taking the time from the Royal yacht, and that the same practice shall prevail as Mr Goschen proposes when the Prince of Wales represents the Queen, of which notice should be given.

The Queen has no wish to interfere with the proper responsibility which should rest on an admiral, but trusts Mr Goschen will feel that at no time can the Queen place herself under the order of an admiral, or the Board of Admiralty.

The Queen thanks Mr Goschen for the manner in which he has treated the question, and well knows he is incapable of acting discourteously to her or any of the Royal Family.

This incident, which began so mildly as a slight difference of opinion between sailors with regard to the interpretation of nebulous regulations, ended in the Cabinet discussing the Queen's supremacy at sea. At one time the controversy threatened to become acute, and on one side were the Prime Minister, the First Lord of the Admiralty, the Cabinet and the Sea Lords of the Admiralty, while on the other side there was only Queen Victoria quite determined not to give away any of her rights at sea.

Finally, in the spring of 1873, the Lords of the Admiralty very solemnly issued a circular in which they 'desired it to be understood' that whenever the Queen or the Prince of Wales were on board the Royal yacht or any of Her Majesty's ships, with Standard flying, 'the regulation firing of the morning and evening gun is to be adhered to . . . but the time is to be taken from the gun which will be fired from the Royal yacht . . .'

The Pony Row, Balmoral, 1869

Life at Balmoral was distinctly quiet in 1869 when Queen Victoria was in retirement and visitors were rare. A Minister or two might come and go; a painter or sculptor might be wanted to execute some memorial; but otherwise there were only the members of the Household. Dullness and a sense of ennui grew until a storm in a teacup seemed inevitable, and such a storm sprang up over the bestriding of ponies by a clergyman, a sculptor and a German secretary. Queen Victoria, although in retirement, kept a very firm hand on all that concerned the Household, and her love of animals made her particularly interested in the kennels and the stables at each of the Royal palaces. Dogs she adored and was rarely unaccompanied by one, but horses and ponies she was also very fond of, and always alluded to them by name. Among her favourites at Balmoral were several sturdy Highland ponies. These ponies are not difficult to ride: in fact no knowledge of horsemanship is necessary, and therefore a man who would never think of attempting to ride a horse or an ordinary pony, mounts a hill pony with the greatest confidence. All he has to do is to sit still and the surefooted animal will take him up and down precipitous places without the slightest trouble.

The man, however, who has had no experience of horses and ponies is no judge of what a pony should and should not do. It was, no doubt, for these reasons that Queen Victoria decided to restrict the pony-riding to those who understood horses, probably having been told stories about the inconsiderate manner in which the ponies were treated. But while she wished to prevent the ponies being ridden by bad riders, she did not wish to hurt her guests' feelings by letting them know that any restrictions emanated from her. This unpleasant duty, therefore, devolved upon the Equerry-in-Waiting, who had charge of all the stables, and it was his duty to see that no carriage, horse, or pony was taken out by people who had not been given the privilege of using them by the Queen. The Equerry-in-Waiting was Colonel Ponsonby, who was not appointed Private Secretary till two years later.

Among the guests at Balmoral in the autumn in 1869 were Canon Duckworth, a friend of the Prince of Wales, who was probably staying at Balmoral because the Queen wished to consult him about the Prince's future, and Mr Edgar Boehm, an eminent sculptor, who was often employed by the Queen.★ In addition, there was Mr Hermann Sahl, the German secretary, whose principal work consisted of drafting official letters of condolence and congratulation to foreign sovereigns.

All these three considered themselves capable of riding hill ponies, but there were members of the Royal family who did not hold this opinion, and late in the August of 1869, Colonel Ponsonby received an intimation that Canon Duckworth, Mr Boehm and Mr Sahl were no longer to be allowed the freedom of the Royal stables. His note of what happened when he informed these gentlemen of this decision runs as follows:

On August 21 I received a message from the Queen to say that irregularities having crept into the stables, she hoped I would give orders as from myself that none were to have ponies except by my especial orders, and that I was not to allow them to be overworked. Next day I received a 'confidential' memorandum saying that Duckworth and Sahl were only to ride on occasions. I told them so. They asked, 'Is this the Queen's order?' I replied, 'You must take it as my order, but you can well understand I give no order without being desired.' This is the point of the controversy. It is said I took on myself to give these orders suppressing the Queen's name. I understood I was not to give her name, but I fully made D. and S. understand that the order came from the Queen. D. accordingly spoke and wrote to me saying he hoped I would protest against this restriction, thus showing by this that he perfectly understood it was

★ Mr Boehm, by birth a Hungarian, settled in London in 1862 and became naturalized. He was elected A.R.A. in 1878 and was created a baronet in 1889. His most notable statues in London are Lord Beaconsfield, Dean Stanley (in Westminster Abbey), Lord Napier of Magdala, Carlyle and William Tyndale, while among his innumerable busts are those of Gladstone, Huxley, Rosebery, Russell, Wolseley and Shaftesbury.

the Queen. As D. could ride but seldom, I saw no difficulty in his applying through me as always used to be the case, and that I did not think there was much possibility of his being refused a pony. I know that Duckworth has felt sore about it, as he considers it a withdrawal of one of his privileges, but I never heard anything more from him. Sahl spoke to me in a half jolly sort of way about it, showing that he understood it was the Queen's order, not my own idea.

On the 31st August I was going out in a hurry and met Sahl, who asked me whether he might have a certain pony, which had always been out, as he was on his way to order ponies for himself and Boehm. I said, 'You know that you must not order ponies for yourself and they will not give them to you without and under orders from me. Neither you nor Boehm can take a pony by right.' Sahl said, 'I assure you, you must have made a mistake about Boehm. The order you received could not be intended to apply to him. Let me submit the question.' I replied, 'By all means if you think it will do any good.' I then gave him an order for the two ponies, but I believe he did not take them. This, I maintain, also proves he knew it was not my order but the Queen's. What he wrote I don't know. But we went to the Gelder Shiel, and there Lady Churchill* told me there was a trouble about the ponies, that someone had complained of this order, and that the Queen had been told that Boehm, who was accustomed to live in a gentleman's house and to have always ponies there, would go home if he had not one at Balmoral. I told Lady Churchill I had seen enough of Boehm to see he was a gentleman and had never sent such a message, and Lady C. quite agreed with me. She then told me the Queen was afraid of Sahl's riding, that he damaged the ponies, but if anyone went with him, he might join expeditions, etc. But he was not to take out Boehm. In view of the above, Boehm might ride out with us sometimes, and I had better ask him to do so. Duckworth might come with us occasionally, when convenient.

Early in September I returned to Balmoral. I asked Boehm to ride, but he was busy and could not. On September 28 I received another message from Lady C. urging me to be very particular in impressing these rules upon people. After luncheon I sent out an order for a dogcart. Sahl came to me and said, 'As you are seeing to the stables, order "Maude" and "Clyde" for me and Boehm.' I have since heard that he came to me after having been told in the stables that ponies

* One of the Queen's favourite ladies-in-waiting.

130

were not given without an order. His style was dictatorial, but not suspecting he was wanting a row, I thought it chaff and said, 'My dear Sahl, I am not supposed to grant you these ponies.' A row followed and he said Duckworth did not mean to protest against this order. Surely these words show he understood the order was the Queen's not mine. He got angry and voluble and rushed away. It is quite true, however, that I did not introduce the Queen's name, because as the instructions respecting Sahl and Boehm were confidential, I could not do so. This is the weak point. As Prince Christian★ says, if you keep the order a secret the blame is applied to you; if you publish it Sahl will be more furious than ever.

On Monday, Sahl sent the most outrageous letter to the Queen, first three pages full of invective about the insolence of Colonel Ponsonby, who refuses him a pony in the ordinary way. Both complain of 'Colonel Ponsonby's manipulating the Household' (Boehm says this is fiction), and Sahl says that ponies are given to footmen and these servants sniff at him, and that he is called in to write the Queen's letters. He concluded by dictating an order that he was to have any pony that was available.

Duckworth does not agree about the annoyance, but he does about the ponies, and says that my manner to Sahl annoyed him.

I begged Prince Christian not to consider me in the matter as Sahl, having written the letter, need not be considered as having offended me. I had no feeling on the subject, for what I had done was to execute the Queen's order to the best of my power.

Sahl wrote, just as I was going, the enclosed letter. By 'the others' I presume he meant Biddulph.†

The 'enclosed letter' from Sahl, to which Colonel Ponsonby refers, must surely be one of the most surprising missives ever received by the Queen's Equerry. Although the military autocracy in Germany was only in its infancy, Mr Sahl had evidently at his home suffered from the fact that he wore no uniform and was unconnected in any way with the Army, but in England such a thing as a military caste was unknown. Still, under the delusion that Colonel Ponsonby had intended to inflict a snub on him personally, he came to the conclusion that this could only be because he was not a soldier, quite oblivious to the fact that neither the canon nor the sculptor was tainted with

★ Son-in-law of Queen Victoria.
† Lieut.-General Sir Thomas Biddulph, Keeper of the Privy Purse.

militarism. It was dated Balmoral, September 30, 1869, and runs as follows:

My dear Ponsonby – Hearing from Duckworth that you are evidently under some misconception regarding my '*outrageous*' letter to the Queen, I cannot help calling your attention to the following points:

You (personally) refused to me (personally) the use of a pony, although you had – as Prince Christian, by the Queen's command, last night assured me – the right and power to grant it, and when allusion was made to the fact that *others* freely obtained *your* permission, your answer was: 'Well, all I can tell you is that I shall not allow it to you.' The *others* happening to be military officers, I could only find one clue to this unsympathetic treatment, viz. a certain military exclusiveness and jealousy towards *non-officers in the Army*; and I maintain up to the present hour that if I had been, *e.g.*, a major – I should have obtained your permission.

I therefore strongly disclaim a translation and interpretation which is not at all justified in using the terms '*military arrogance and insolence*' which I earnestly beg to substitute by the words *jealousy* and *exclusiveness*.

Further on, as my *soreness* on this *ground* was only a personal one, I cannot possibly allow your version, which speaks of the *whole Household annoyance* at your military arrogance as you say! as, besides the ladies, I am (with Duckworth) the only civilian concerned!

But, as to your withholding *your permission to me*, I *beg* to say I *have* the *fullest sympathy* of all those with whom I already spoke on the subject, and am perfectly sure I shall obtain it equally from all who get a fair statement of the facts.

As I shall have no opportunity in all probability to see you before your going, I avail myself of this opportunity of saying goodbye to you and Mrs Ponsonby. Yours sincerely,

Hermann Sahl.

P.S. – There is no objection against showing this reply to Prince Christian.

Prince Christian now found himself in a very difficult position. Being an independent-minded man who was fearless in expressing his opinion, he naturally came to the conclusion that Canon Duckworth and Mr Sahl had been badly treated when he heard their version of the story, but being too much a man of the world to commit himself entirely without hearing the other side, he approached the Equerry, Colonel Ponsonby. He then learnt that it was really the Queen behind all this, and while sympathizing with their complaint he naturally felt it his duty to support Her Majesty's authority.

It was about this date (September 30) that Colonel Ponsonby received the following letter from Canon Duckworth:

My dear Ponsonby – I can assure you that I have been entirely misrepresented if it has been insinuated that I have the slightest complaint to make of *you personally*, or that I have ever found your manner other than thoroughly courteous and kind to me. I am exceedingly sorry that Sahl should have conveyed such an impression to you.

My sympathy with him extends to this recent restriction in the use of the ponies, of which, of course, I am at liberty to form my own opinion, and, as you know, I did not shrink from expressing it frankly to you at the earliest moment.

I can assure you that against yourself personally I have not the slightest feeling; and Sahl is utterly mistaken in quoting me as one aggrieved by 'military arrogance'. He himself appears to have been deeply affronted by the manner of denial of a little privilege which I can testify he has been as careful as myself not to abuse, and which I do think it was a very great mistake to withdraw. The harmony and comfort of those who are serving the Queen from year's end to year's end is surely worth while, with stables full of ponies. – Yours very truly,

R. Duckworth.

Meanwhile, Colonel Ponsonby had sent 'the soft answer that turneth away wrath', and Mr Sahl's reply (dated October 1, 1869) runs as follows:

I am pleased to see that you always looked upon me as a *friend*; I may add in return, that it was also my constant endeavour to prove to you and Mrs Ponsonby that I fully appreciated your friendship – any interruption of it I greatly regret. But with regard to this miserable matter of the *ponies* and your speaking of my *accusations*, I must, first of all, remind you of *your own advice* given to me in August 'to protest if I chose'.

The deeper cause of my irritation has to do with a matter far too delicate to be treated in a letter; perhaps a mere *allusion* is intelligible; if not, I trust I shall, at some later period, have an opportunity to talk the matter over with you.

Let me conclude by saying that when making my protest I strongly felt that what I did was done in the interest of the *whole Household* certainly as much as in my own! All who know me here are aware that I have no private aims in view.

Hermann Sahl.

The next day (October 2) the excellent canon, as became his cloth, tried to smooth matters without, however, weakening in his support of his co-equestrians, the German secretary and the sculptor. The amusing part of the squabble was that if either of these three had been asked to mount a *horse* none of them would have dared do so. The sculptor seems to have been singularly silent; whether it was from apathy or from a shrewd suspicion that he was up against a far higher authority than the Equerry-in-Waiting can only be surmised. Canon Duckworth's letter ran:

My dear Ponsonby – Sahl had written to you yesterday before your letter from Ballater reached me, or he would have explained to you what is now apparent to him, that you have been much misinformed as to a large portion of his letter to the Queen.

Sahl declares he had not the remotest thought of being *dictatorial* in asking you to order ponies for Boehm and himself. And as you had *volunteered* to supply Boehm with a pony, he thought there would be no difficulty. And when you absolutely declined to grant his request, he says he did not ask you if you *would* protest against the order, but expressed his astonishment and disappointment that you *had not done so*, supposing, what he says you declined to admit, that the order was not your own, but imposed from a higher quarter.

Certain it is that, whatever may have been the nature of your interview, I never saw Sahl so irritated and excited in my life as when I met him by chance downstairs a few minutes afterwards. I asked in amazement what had happened, and he then told me with strong indignation of the rebuff he had received. What annoyed him was nothing 'rude' or 'coarse' in your manner, he assures me, but the *marked personal exception*, which you were at no pains to disguise, made to *his* case, and which you would not account for.

Sahl is very much cut up by this whole affair. As he is a most kind-hearted man, and has always been on very friendly terms with you, I am sure that estrangement from you is deeply painful to him. Whatever may be thought of his letter, I am confident that, though written with wounded feelings, it was not intended as the *personal attack* it has appeared to be. So I earnestly hope that this unhappy business may be forgotten, and good feeling restored.

With many apologies for the length of this letter, believe me, yours sincerely,

R. Duckworth.

To this letter Colonel Ponsonby replied on October 5. Unfortunately, the actual letter he sent is not available, but from a rough note left by him it is evident that he took up the cudgels with vigour. 'The persons aimed at,' he wrote, 'were not civilians – the order was applied to all; hence there was no inequality of treatment. If footmen have given orders I will, of course, investigate.' But he added that he did not 'know any house where any man may take any pony at any time without the leave of the Master of the house. You say it wasn't my manner. Before, you said it was, hence my Ballater letter. How can you think that the order is a personal one when you say that it is against civilians? In any case, I am the Queen's servant, and the order was that no one should have a pony without my permission. Generally speaking, I should have given you one if you had asked me.

'Sahl claims the right to take any pony at any time out of the stables without reference to Equerry. I say according to rule he cannot do so.'

Three days later (on October 8), Canon Duckworth, finding he was on a bad wicket, had recourse to a verbose and intricate explanation of what he meant in his first letter:

My dear Ponsonby – I must thank you for your kind letter from Hampton Court. I cordially join with you in the hope that this misunderstanding between Sahl and yourself is at an end, and that you may be friends as of old. I need not explain again *my* share in the matter, as you are well aware that there has been no interruption in my friendly feeling towards you, and I trust there never will be.

Suppose that Sahl, whose control of the library corresponds to the Equerry's control of the stables, had said to me, 'I am going to be very strict about the use of the library: the books are to be much less used than they have been, and I shall only give leave to take them out under the most exceptional circumstances.' I should have felt no little disgust at such an announcement. And if, on applying to him for a book, he had absolutely declined to let me have it, and refused to give his reason for doing so, I think I should then have addressed the Queen on the subject, and should have asked her whether *she* really intended to withdraw from me a privilege which I had for my part been careful never to abuse.

I would not have you think that I asked you to take a course disrespectful to the Queen when I suggested to you to 'protest' at first. Of course, I did not mean that you should do more than ask to have the order reconsidered for our sakes. I don't dispute for one moment your right to judge for yourself of the expediency in this case. I only wish to assure you that I had no thought of asking you to do anything either disrespectful or impracticable. And I was perfectly sure that you were little likely to have had any hand in bringing about the change deprecated. I hope you won't imagine that there is any feeling of antipathy towards you here, for there is nothing of the kind.

With my kind regards, believe me, dear Ponsonby, yours very sincerely,

R. Duckworth.

The matter now seemed to be settled in the most amicable manner, but its real funeral dirge was sung three weeks later, on November 1, 1869, when Mr Hermann Sahl, in writing to Colonel Ponsonby about the Librarian's post in the Royal Library, took occasion to add an apology. It is curious to note that Sahl was never told that it was the Queen's order, and was therefore left under the impression that Colonel Ponsonby had taken upon himself to forbid people to ride. His letter ran:

> My dear Ponsonby – I am ashamed to say that I have received a letter from you, without having replied to the first – which solely referred to the miserable pony question. I daresay you hardly expected an answer and are (as much as I am) anxious to bury the squabble. I will therefore say nothing more, but correct *one incorrect* statement of *mine*, to which you call justly my attention. I was wrong in speaking of *others* who had obtained *your* permission to ride; I ought to have spoken simply of *others* (if I chose to use the plural form at all) *having obtained the Equerries'* permission.
>
> I am very sorry for having made this mistake, but I trust this frank confession and correction will persuade you to forget the original error, and help to convince you, that in the whole of this matter there was *no* animosity on my part against you, as I shall be able – I hope soon – to show you when you give me an opportunity to *talk* the subject over.
>
> Hermann Sahl.

Queen Victoria, who undoubtedly was kept fully informed by Lady Churchill of all that had passed, must have been very much amused at this storm in a tea-cup, but she had saved her dear hill ponies from any possible harm, and that, to her, was far more important than the wounded feelings of her guests.

Mr Gladstone's Retirement, 1894

In 1894 Mr Gladstone was eighty-five, and although his mind was as active as ever, certain defects of sight and hearing – slight, but sufficient to be a handicap in parliamentary work – led him to contemplate retirement. Such a decision was easily made, but the most serious obstacles were obvious when the question came to be considered as to who should succeed him as Prime Minister and Leader of the Liberal Party. He himself seemed to have expressed no opinion, probably because he was never asked to do so, but the intelligentsia of the Liberal Party supported Lord Rosebery, then Foreign Secretary, and a still larger body of Liberals were firmly of the opinion that a Prime Minister in the House of Lords was an anachronism in those democratic times – especially as it was the Liberal Party that was involved, and they, in turn, supported the claims of Sir William Harcourt, who held the post of Chancellor of the Exchequer.

The fact that Queen Victoria cordially disliked Gladstone is now well known: in fact she herself never made any secret of her antipathy to him in her later years. According to the late Lord Gladstone her relations with his father were of the most friendly description to begin with, and it was not until Disraeli appeared on the scene that she began to dislike him. This, Lord Gladstone maintains, was entirely due to Disraeli, who poisoned her mind systematically against the Grand Old Man. Some people, however, thought this was owing to the fact that while Disraeli flattered and amused her, Gladstone lectured her and addressed her as if she were a public meeting.

Her opinion of Gladstone is very forcibly given in a letter which she wrote to Lord Lansdowne, when he was Viceroy of India, on August 12, 1892. The General Election of the preceding June had resulted in the overthrow of Lord Salisbury's Government and in the return of Mr Gladstone to power with a majority of forty, which included seventy-two Irish Nationalists. The new Parliament met for the first time on August 4.

Her letter ran:

> The Queen-Empress has to thank the Viceroy for his letter of the 27th June.
>
> She feels more than ever at this painful, anxious moment when, by an incomprehensible, reckless vote, the result of most unfair and abominable misrepresentation at the elections, one of the best and most useful Governments has been defeated, how important it is to have so able and reliable a Viceroy in India.
>
> The Queen-Empress can hardly trust herself to say what she feels and thinks on the subject. Apart from the pain of parting from some great personal friends and people whom she can trust and rely on, the danger to the country, to Europe, to her vast Empire, which is involved in having all these great interests entrusted to the shaking hand of an old, wild, and incomprehensible man of eighty-two and a half, is very great! It is a terrible trial, but, thank God, the country is sound, and it cannot last. The Gladstonian majority is quite divided, and solely depends on the Irish vote.*

Rumours of Mr Gladstone's retirement began to circulate in the January of 1894, which the usual official denial rapidly confirmed. Mr Gladstone was then at Biarritz. He returned on February 10. 'His colleagues,' as Morley notes, 'carried almost to importunity their appeals to him to stay; to postpone what one of them called this "moment of anguish".' But Gladstone had by now made up his mind, although as he noted in one of his private memoranda a month later, 'Politics are like a labyrinth, from the inner intricacies of which it is even more difficult to escape than it was to find the way into them.' His age and his infirmities brought him on February 17 to express a wish to see Sir Henry Ponsonby 'not later than Friday' and 'earlier rather than later'. Two days later Mr Gladstone wrote to Sir Henry:

> If, as I understand, the Queen's coming up is fixed for Thursday, you, I conclude, will move from Osborne on that day, and perhaps you could make that the day for calling on me at any hour you like to name, as it will probably be a blank day at the House of Commons.

On February 24 Mr Gladstone, as Sir Henry noted, 'came to Buckingham Palace at eleven, and told me that his desire to see the Queen affected his retirement and that he did not want it to get out before Parliament was over. Could it be kept quiet?'

* Published in Lord Newton's *Life of Lord Lansdowne*.

That same day Sir Henry Ponsonby wrote to Mr Gladstone, and kept the following rough note of his letter:

> I repeated to the Queen the substance of my conversation with you. Her Majesty asked what was the message you desired to give her. I of course said I knew nothing. Her Majesty replied that she could not bind herself to preserve secrecy on a matter of which she knew nothing and asked for some hint. This I explained I could again get from you. Her Majesty observed that if it related to Parliament she could not promise not to consult several persons.
>
> I did not feel capable of discussing this question, and I promised to repeat to you what Her Majesty had said.

On the same day Sir Henry also wrote to Sir Algernon West, who was then private secretary to Mr Gladstone:

> The Queen said she would not bind herself to any secrecy about matters where she must consult friends. Was it dissolution? – of course I would not say. All I could say was that I would ask him. She won't, she says, agree to keep secret some dark proposal he may make.

Mr Gladstone's reply was as follows:

> Thanks for your letter.
>
> The very last thing I should pray for or claim is discussion on my notice or intimation. I should deem it wholly premature. For this reason I contemplated a letter and one not requiring acknowledgement.
>
> If Her Majesty, on the other hand, enjoins a personal statement, which seemingly entails a day's delay, of course I will cheerfully obey.
>
> *If* I am to write perhaps you will kindly let me know.

Friday now passed, and the Queen's fear that Mr Gladstone might inveigle her into some sort of 'secret discussion' had proved groundless. It was plain that she thought that if Mr Gladstone had something to say to her of great importance there was no need why it should be treated so secretly, or why he should not beforehand give her some indication of his opinion. The next day Sir Henry Ponsonby wrote to Mr Gladstone:

> I could not get a very clear reply last night and indeed even now I cannot give a brief answer. The Queen said she feared that entering into a secret discussion with you might cause misunderstandings and that she would wish to be able to consult other friends.
>
> I pointed out that in your letter you did not ask her to express any opinion and that you did not even ask for an acknowledgement, and therefore I asked whether a brief personal interview would not be best. The Queen said that if you did not expect her to do more in this matter than simply to listen, this might be so. But I

should make it quite clear that Her Majesty should not be expected to discuss the matter. If so, the Queen could listen to you upon the subject when she sees you.

By this time, of course, the cat was well out of the bag. Everybody who was anybody – and a good many nobodies – knew that Mr Gladstone was going to resign. Only Mr Gladstone and the Queen seemed to be in any doubt as to the correct manner in which his resignation should be effected. The following day (February 27) the Queen wrote to Sir Henry Ponsonby:

> The Queen hears from the Duke of Connaught (who asked her what it meant) that it is placarded everywhere and is posted up at the clubs that Mr Gladstone is going to resign. Others have also asked and she only said she knew nothing, but thought there must be something 'in the air'.
>
> Is the Queen not right in believing that when a Prime Minister resigns the Government is broken up? – of course, if one of them wishes to succeed him he must re-form and support the Government. This was done in '65 when Lord Palmerston died and Lord Russell was appointed.
>
> The secret which Mr Gladstone makes so much of, is constantly leaking out – in spite of all his great fuss and anxiety about secrecy.

The Queen had just sent this letter to Sir Henry when she received the following note from him: 'Would Your Majesty wish to see Mr Gladstone at three o'clock tomorrow?' 'She had better see him tomorrow,' replied the Queen, 'but it would be more courteous to acknowledge his letter and say she would see him at three. What is the Queen to say to her family, who will ask her, and to Lord Rosebery and the Chancellor?'

Hardly had the Queen sent the note than she received the following letter from Mr Gladstone, which is dated February 27:

> Mr Gladstone presents his humble duty to Your Majesty, and believes himself now authorized to convey to Your Majesty the preliminary intimation which he has thought it would be for the convenience of Your Majesty to receive.
>
> It is to the effect that, when the business of the present Session, and any matter immediately connected therewith, shall have been disposed of, he believes it will be his duty to tender to Your Majesty, on physical grounds, his resignation of office.
>
> As his present object is simply to inform Your Majesty, without asking or desiring even a formal acknowledgement of this letter, he reserves all explanation of particulars until the day, perhaps a very early one, when he humbly proposes to carry his intention into effect.

The next afternoon (February 28) Queen Victoria gave an audience to Mr Gladstone, 'who indirectly conveyed to the Queen what she might soon expect to learn from him'. He afterwards told Mr Morley (then Chief Secretary for Ireland) that he derived the impression that the Sovereign would not seek his advice as to a successor.

Meanwhile, the Queen feared that the formation of a new Government would interfere with her plans for a holiday, and that she would either have to curtail or abandon her projected visit to Florence. That day she wrote to Sir Henry Ponsonby:

Buckingham Palace.

The Queen was asked no question about Lord Rosebery being unwilling, and on the contrary talked of future arrangements. If only it could be tided over till the Queen returns, or else the little rest and benefit she has looked forward to will be ruined; and this long-suffering and pain makes her very worn-out. If there is a change of Government it will take a fortnight or three weeks, and we ought to go on the 13th – Tuesday fortnight – and the day will be too short. Can Sir Henry not do something? To go so far for only three weeks would be useless almost.

The question as to who should succeed Mr Gladstone had now reached a point when some definite decision should be made. The situation was aptly described by Sir Edward Hamilton, who had been private secretary to Mr Gladstone, and who now wrote to Sir Henry Ponsonby on February 28:

I have generally troubled you with my remarks in times of crisis; so I hope you won't object to a few lines on the present occasion. They may be useful to you, for I think I know pretty well the lie of the political land; and I know you won't betray my indiscretion.

Everything would be quite smooth sailing if it were not for our great difficulty – I mean our big friend Harcourt; and as I am very much attached to him personally I regret more than I can say that he should constitute the difficulty. But for him, I am certain that every member of the present Cabinet would rally round and joyfully serve under Rosebery. Rosebery is the only man really competent to be the Queen's Prime Minister. His colleagues (with that one exception) feel that; and he would inspire confidence among all right-minded citizens. But the two questions which have to be looked in the face are:

(1) Will Harcourt submit to serve under Rosebery, and

(2) If he would so submit, would Rosebery be content to take him as his deputy with the lead in the House of Commons.

I doubt if either of these questions can be answered in the affirmative; and there is no doubt that among the Radicals he will be strongly backed. They only know him as a fine fighting Parliamentarian. They have no experience of him as a colleague. This feeling enhances the difficulty of the situation.

It looks, therefore, as if the problem could only be solved in two ways, either by the supersession of H. in the House of Commons, which would be very awkward, or by the formation of the Government under another man than R., like Kimberley, who would be less frightened at having H. as leader in the Commons and be better able to pull with him.

This, I believe, pretty accurately describes the state of affairs.

There is one other point to which I should like to allude, and it is this: I take it that the man for whom, according to general expectation, the Queen will send, is Rosebery. But it occurs to me that in his own interests as well as those of the Crown it might be well that in the first instance the man sent for should be Kimberley as present leader of the House of Lords. He would be sure to say he must defer to Rosebery; and by this move it could not be said that Rosebery was selected as the Crown's nominee.

It is all very interesting; and I hope somehow or other the difficulties which I foresee may be surmounted and the right man be put in the right place.

The next day (March 1) Mr Gladstone held his last Cabinet Council. His biographer, Lord Morley, describes the scene:

Mr Gladstone sat composed and still as marble; and the emotion of the Cabinet did not gain him for an instant. He followed the words of acknowledgement and farewell in a little speech of four or five minutes, his voice unbroken and serene, the tone low, grave and steady . . . Then, hardly above a breath, but every accent heard, he said 'God bless you all' . . . and went out of one door, while his colleagues, with minds oppressed, filed out of the other. In his diary he enters: 'A really moving scene'.

A little later in the afternoon he made his last speech in the House, striking a 'note of passion' and speaking 'with rising fire'. He sat down amidst the vehement plaudits of his followers, who were not supposed to know that this was his last speech as Prime Minister.

The next day Lord Rosebery received through the Prince of Wales a message from the Queen to the effect that she would like to see him at Windsor to ascertain whether he would be prepared to succeed Mr Gladstone.

His reply to Sir Henry Ponsonby ran as follows:

Foreign Office,
Secret.   March 2, 1894.

My dear Ponsonby – I have received the Queen's gracious message through the Prince of Wales. It would not be proper, I conceive, that I should address her on the subject of it, so I write to you with the intention that you should send this letter to her.

It would be affectation to deny that I have often seen it suggested that I might succeed Mr Gladstone when he should retire. In view of that I have kept myself sedulously in the background. I have not made a speech or written a line for publication. I have done this deliberately to avoid this *damnosa hereditas*. And I delivered the only speech that I did make (that on the Irish Government Bill) in the full hope and expectation that it would put an end to any question of my leading a Liberal Government.

My reasons are these:

(1) I am altogether unfitted for the post, as regards capacity and knowledge.

(2) I am in an office where I believe I can do good work and where a change just now might do harm. Why then should I be taken out of a round hole and put into a square one?

(3) The House of Commons is justly jealous of the leadership of a Liberal peer.

The Liberal Prime Minister, if a peer, will be dependent entirely on the leader of the House of Commons. While the House of Commons is settling the affairs of the country under its leader, the Prime Minister will be shut up in an enemy's prison with an intrepid band of trusty followers.

The Radical cave announcement last night, though not, I believe, formidable in itself, is right in this – that a Liberal peer, as Prime Minister, is in a wholly false position. He cannot control the House of Commons or his representative there, he can only watch them from the Strangers' Gallery.

(4) I am very sceptical as to the apparent movement in my favour. It is, I believe, negative, and rises much more from dislike and distrust of one of my colleagues than from anything personal to me. In this anxiety to avoid him, they can see no issue or chance of safety but through me.

These are the objections I see and which I express without reserve, for I think it my duty to make the Queen aware of them.

Believe me, yours sincerely,

R.

We glory in our nebulous Constitution, but the question whether the Sovereign of this country acts on anyone's advice in the selection of a Prime Minister seems to have been skilfully avoided by constitutional theorists. Obviously, when a Prime Minister is hopelessly beaten at an election, his advice cannot be sought when the Opposition comes into power. The case is, however, quite different when the Prime Minister resigns and his party remains in power. The only question to be decided in that case is upon which of his colleagues his mantle is to fall, and there can be little doubt that he himself must be one of the best judges.

Is this a case where possibly the Sovereign can do wrong? The correct interpretation of this seems to be that any Minister can be selected who is able to form a Government and who is therefore prepared to defend the action of the Sovereign in Parliament.

In the case of Gladstone, Queen Victoria had no intention of asking his advice. Neither did he ever imagine she would do so. Whether he would have recommended Rosebery, Harcourt or Kimberley must therefore remain a matter of conjecture.* Harcourt had strong claims,

* Lord Morley states that he would have preferred Lord Spencer.

for he had been leader of the House of Commons in Gladstone's absence and had borne the great burden of the day. Some Liberals thought that as he might refuse to serve under Lord Rosebery it would be best to have Lord Kimberley or perhaps Lord Spencer. Mr Labouchere attempted to raise a revolt amongst the rank and file of the Liberal Party against a peer Prime Minister, and wrote a strongly worded protest to *The Times*, urging Sir William Harcourt's claims and questioning the Queen's right to make it what he termed a Court appointment, but he received little support.

On March 2, Mr Gladstone, accompanied by Mrs Gladstone, was invited to stay at Windsor Castle by Queen Victoria. As they drove to Paddington Station from Downing Street they were affectionately greeted by a large crowd, and on arrival at Windsor Station they had quite an ovation. They dined with the Queen that night, but probably the conversation was general and nothing was said about the political situation.

The next day (March 3) a Council was held for the prorogation of Parliament. Mr Gladstone was, of course, already at Windsor and the following Ministers were summoned from London: Lord Kimberley, Lord President of the Council; Lord Rosebery, Secretary of State for Foreign Affairs; Sir William Harcourt, Chancellor of the Exchequer; Lord Ripon, Secretary of State for the Colonies; and Lord Spencer, First Lord of the Admiralty. In addition to these, Lord Acton was present as Lord-in-Waiting. Lord Acton was a man of encyclopaedic knowledge, but, like many erudite scholars, was inclined to be absent-minded – a circumstance which had a curious result.

Meanwhile, the secret as to who should be invited to follow Mr Gladstone had been so well kept that apparently, with the exception of Lord Rosebery, none of the Ministers knew whom the Queen had selected. According to the usual procedure the Ministers were shown into one of the drawing-rooms, while the Queen waited in an adjoining room where the Council was to be held. The Lord-in-Waiting ushered in the six Ministers and the Council was held. At the conclusion, the Queen asked Mr Gladstone to remain while the others retired, and he tendered his resignation, which (according to the Court Circular) was graciously accepted by Her Majesty.

His formal letter of resignation ran as follows:

10 Downing Street, Whitehall.

Mr Gladstone presents his most humble duty to Your Majesty.

The close of the Session, and the approach of a new one, have offered Mr Gladstone a suitable opportunity for considering the condition of his sight and hearing, both of them impaired, in relation to his official obligations. As they now place serious, and also growing, obstacles in the way of the efficient discharge of those obligations, the result has been that he has found it his duty humbly to tender to Your Majesty his resignation of the high offices which Your Majesty has been pleased to entrust to him. He desires to make this surrender accompanied with a grateful sense of the condescending kindness which Your Majesty has graciously shown him on so many occasions during the various periods for which he has had the honour to serve Your Majesty.

Mr Gladstone will not suddenly burden Your Majesty with a recital of particulars. He may, however, say that, although at eighty-four years of age he is sensible of a diminished capacity for prolonged labour, this is not in itself such as would justify his praying to be relieved from the restraints and exigencies of official life. But his deafness has become, in Parliament, and even in the Cabinet, a serious inconvenience, of which he must reckon on some progress to an increase. More grave than this, and more rapid in its growth, is the obstruction of vision, which arises from cataract in both his eyes. It has cut him off in substance from the newspapers, and from all except the best types in the best lights, while, even as to them, he cannot master them with that ordinary facility and dispatch which he deems absolutely requisite for the due dispatch of his public duties. In other respects than reading, the operation of the complaint is not as yet so serious; but this one he deems to be vital.

Accordingly, he brings together these two facts, the condition of his sight and hearing, and the break in the course of public affairs brought about in the ordinary way by the close of the Session. He has therefore felt that this is the fitting opportunity for the resignation, which by this letter he humbly prays Your Majesty to accept.*

March 3rd, 1894

For the moment, Mr Gladstone thought that the Queen was going to 'break down', but she rallied herself, and there followed a conversation which was 'neither here nor there'. The Queen thanked Gladstone again for a little service he had done for her in the case of the Duke of Coburg – probably one of the smallest incidents of his four premierships. They spoke of oculists – and Mrs Gladstone – but never a word regarding the successorship to the Prime Ministership. A halting moment or two passed, and then a 'kind and warm farewell'.

This is Gladstone's own account of the interview, related by him to Morley – but how true it is no one knows. Gladstone was over eighty, deaf, and going blind, besides being considerably upset at his farewell to public life. It seems almost inconceivable that the Queen should

* Published in Morley's *Life of Gladstone*, vol. iii. p 388.

have talked of such trivial matters on an occasion like this – yet her account of the interview is missing: or perhaps was never written down.

When Mr Gladstone left the room, a moment of intense and almost dramatic interest arose for the Ministers waiting in the anteroom, who were soon to see whom the Queen had selected to succeed Mr Gladstone. The Queen now told Lord Acton to bring in Lord Rosebery, but she may have spoken low and he did not hear what she said, or possibly he may have been so sure she would send for Sir William Harcourt that he took it for granted that this was her choice. In any case he retired from the Council room and asked Sir William Harcourt to come in to the Queen. Naturally, Harcourt assumed that he was going to be asked to form a Government, and walked sedately into the Council Chamber. What Lord Rosebery's feelings must have been to see his rival summoned after he had been given to understand by the Prince of Wales that he was to be Prime Minister can better be imagined than described.

But his astonishment was nothing compared to the Queen's when having, as she thought, summoned Lord Rosebery, she saw Sir William Harcourt enter the room. Certainly most people would have found the situation most embarrassing, but not for a moment was she at all disconcerted. She merely said that there had been some mistake, and she hoped Sir William would retire again while she spoke to Lord Acton. Whether she told Lord Acton what she thought of him, history does not relate, but she asked him to bring in Lord Rosebery, who was thereupon offered and accepted the post of Prime Minister.

That evening Sir Henry Ponsonby wrote to Mr Gladstone informing him that Lord Rosebery had been appointed Prime Minister in his place. Gladstone's letter in reply, written when he was dispirited and saddened by his eclipse, may well give the final touch to this chapter. Undoubtedly Gladstone would have preferred to have died in harness, and there is perhaps a touch of bitterness in his desire to be treated as 'one of the public'. His letter ran:

10 Downing Street, Whitehall,
March 4th 1894.

Dear Sir H. Ponsonby – I really was ashamed last night at your quickness in writing to me when you are under such pressure, locomotive and other, and when it is I who have been the means of bringing it upon you. Pray take no more trouble and let me take my chance as one of the public. Interesting as all intelligence is under the circumstances, it is probably better that for the time at any rate I should remain an extraneous person. And with many thanks for all your goodness and kindness, I remain, sincerely yours,

W.E. Gladstone.